Advanc [barcode: T0407912] *ed*

"*Born Sacred: Poems for Palestine* is a profound work of grace and solidarity, rooted in a hard-earned understanding of colonialism's insatiable appetite. What Smokii Sumac has done, over the course of 100 searing, open-hearted poems, is give voice to the immeasurable grief of bearing witness to genocide—the overwhelming magnitude of it, colliding with a knowledge that this has happened before, that there is an age-old methodology to the act of endless taking. I am so grateful for this work, for this beautiful, honest reminder that, whatever power empires wield, we have what it can never take. We have one another."

— **OMAR EL AKKAD**, author of *What Strange Paradise*

"The succinct starkness of Smokii Sumac's offerings are an X-Ray to the grief and absurdity of our times. This dangerous dichotomy of trying to live one's everyday life while holding the tragedy of everyday loss is profoundly captured in each stanza."

— **CATHERINE HERNANDEZ**, author and screenwriter of *Scarborough*,

"This collection is the antidote to the silence and cowardice of millions, and the medicine for those who watched the first recorded genocide unfold and needed to be seen and witnessed. Creating room for collective grief, Smokii Sumac shows us the responsibility and power of the poet to face the blank page in the here and now and the necessity for words to remain as a testimony to history. *Born Sacred* is an essential work in the fight for collective liberation and a reminder that hope can be rooted in allyship."

— **RAYYA LIEBICH**, author of *Min Hayati*

"I am always drawn to the constellational consciousness that permeates so many Asian refugee, Indigenous, and Black literary and cultural works. This constellational consciousness, the culturally-informed relational view of life and solidarity in struggle, is vital in Smokii Sumac's collection. In both form and content, the poems shatter dominating linear and compartmentalizing interpretations of the world with constellating stanzas, voices, and experiences that reveal the intertwined histories and presents of colonial harm and Indigenous survivance.

— **MARAL AGUILERA-MORADIPOUR**, Simon Fraser University

BORN SACRED

POEMS FOR PALESTINE

WRITTEN BY

Smokii Sumac

FOREWORD BY

Zaynab Mohammed

Roseway Publishing
an imprint of Fernwood Publishing
Halifax & Winnipeg

Development editing: Jazz Cook
Copyediting: Emilia Morgan
Cover design: Evan Marnoch
Text design: Lauren Jeanneau
Printed and bound in Canada

Published by Roseway Publishing
an imprint of Fernwood Publishing
Halifax and Winnipeg
2970 Oxford Street, Halifax, Nova Scotia, B3L 2W4
www.fernwoodpublishing.ca/roseway

Fernwood Publishing Company Limited gratefully acknowledges the
financial support of the Government of Canada through the Canada Book
Fund and the Canada Council for the Arts. We acknowledge the Province
of Manitoba for support through the Manitoba Publishers Marketing
Assistance Program and the Book Publishing Tax Credit. We acknowledge
the Nova Scotia Department of Communities, Culture and Heritage for
support through the Publishers Assistance Fund.

Library and Archives Canada Cataloguing in Publication
Title: Born sacred : poems for Palestine / written by Smokii Sumac ;
foreword by Zaynab Mohammed.
Names: Sumac, Smokii, 1988- author | Mohammed, Zaynab,
writer of foreword.
Identifiers: Canadiana 20240537440 | ISBN 9781773637259 (softcover)
Subjects: LCGFT: Poetry.
Classification: LCC PS8637.U569 B67 2025 | DDC C811/.6—dc23

This collection is dedicated to Palestinian and Indigenous life.

FOREWORD

POEMS, IN MY PERSPECTIVE, ARE PRAYERS. They are offerings of solace. They are subtle, yet loud reminders that carry seeds of hope, wonder, connection and possibility. They defy gravity. They have the power to rip our hearts open, turning them inside out. When I look around in our "western world" and beyond, I see many vacant, void and empty hearts. Fear, comfort and complacency have locked some people into a desensitized reality of separation. Poetry, then, is one of the most needed medicines of our times.

Maybe I am wrong. Maybe I don't give the world and its inhabitants enough credit. I am also affected by the state of the world and can't imagine who I could be if I didn't feel fear and pain regularly. As a person who is sensitive beyond desire, I sense hopelessness and indifference more often than not in others and unfortunately, at times, in myself.

What Smokii has done here, writing these poems for Palestine, has been a refuge for many of us during the first months of the genocide in Gaza. The people who are affected from this war machine, that is everyone on the planet, are on some level in a state of shock and disbelief.

If you are not, then I ask you, where is your humanity?

The bloodshed continues. The destruction is mind bending. Famine has set in. Even when the bombs stop, the war will not be over. Palestine has been under occupation for decades. However, it has been more than 100 years since a British man wrote the Balfour Declaration handing over Palestine to Zionists.

As poets, artists and humans, we are entrenched in responsibility to ourselves, our communities and the earth. This is how I see life. We all have a duty in our lives to share our gifts from within us as best as we can. I pray we all discover what we have in us to give and give it with minimal doubt or hesitation. Simplicity is at the heart of this equation.

Smokii has the gift of weaving words into poems and prayers and has done so in this powerful collection. He has kept this window through time open. A window for all those who may be too young to witness the details of the destruction of Gaza. A frame for all those who are indifferent, who don't know how or don't want to witness apartheid in real time. A means for all those who have not looked away from this genocide to grieve and reflect. These poems capture this moment for us, wait for when we are ready to see the truth, and encourage us to lean into each other in rage, grief, horror and commitment to continue to show up despite societal indifference.

It is never too late to change heart or to let our hearts be ripped open. I know this is not something most people have learned in their lives. If we don't have examples of people who are vulnerable, strong and walk with dignity, how will we grow into people like this? I mention this because these poems will awaken your heart in a way that may feel unbearable. And for this, I want you to know that it has been unbearable for all of us who choose to walk with our hearts open.

Every time I reveal myself through my own poems, I think, "there I go again." I want to live a private, simple life. Yet I cannot afford to sit silent on the sidelines. And neither should you. We all have power that fuels us. Yet we let the systems we are entrenched in rob us of our power. It's an automatic happenstance until we realize what is happening.

Have you heard the line, "we are not freeing Palestine, Palestine is freeing us?"

This is the first ever live-streamed genocide in the history of time. People usually learn about genocides after they happen. How many people have you seen murdered, blown up, ripped to pieces, heads blown off, burnt to ash, decomposed into skeletons? How many children's ribs have you witnessed on their frail starved bodies? Can you imagine dying of starvation while the rest of the world has access to food? How many buildings have you seen bombed, blown up, made into rubble, hollowed out, homes and memories destroyed in an instant? How many soldiers have we seen make a mockery of themselves, by posting videos wearing thongs of people they've murdered, revealing their ignorant flaws, highlighting their lack of humanity? How many families have been wiped off the face of the planet in this genocide? Too many. It is too much. We have had enough. And yet the war machine continues.

What have you learned from this genocide?

Truth is deflected. Our politicians are gaslighting us. As is mainstream media. Shame on them.

The double standards and hypocrisy of our time have revealed themselves, clearer than ever. No one can deny this anymore. Despite how easily manipulated we are, we can educate ourselves and take back our power. Accountability is a prayer many of us are on our knees calling in.

It's overwhelming when I look at the corruption of this world. Why was I born with such a caring heart? Why can't I turn off the love I feel for this world? This may be the price of being an artist, as it is my duty to reflect the world I see with my artistic practice. Smokii knows this and does this too.

The words you will read in this book come from a very sensitive person. This person took time out of their day to try to understand a catastrophe happening on the other side of the world.

Separation is a veil I hope we can rip off our eyes and begin to truly see what is before us and the tasks at hand. Palestinians are helping us realize and remember our inherent connection to life and all that is alive. Palestine is freeing us.

Smokii's generous gift of word embroidery in this poetry collection is a testament to solidarity in action. Thank you Smokii for inviting us into your sacred prayers.

May these poems give us permission to feel our shattered hearts. May they give us space to express our grief. May they inspire our gifts as individuals while continuously connecting to our communities. May they open a way for love to shine through, inside and out. May they ignite passion and determination for honoring life's sacredness. May they pull us towards the tasks of being who we are and doing what we are here to do. May they remind us that we are *born sacred.* May these poems add rhythm to our heartbeat. May these poems move us all in to action. May these poems for Palestine be poems for the liberation of all oppressed peoples on this planet. May these poems change what needs changing inside of us. May these poems bring us closer together.

And in doing so, may we become a "we" once again, from the rivers to the seas.

— **ZAYNAB MOHAMMED**, Poet, Storyteller, Artist

PREFACE

TODAY IS OCTOBER 8th, 2024. I do not know how to tell you of what it felt waking up this morning. Yesterday's date marked one year since October 7th, 2023, a date that many of us remember as marking the events leading to the escalation of genocide in Gaza. This preface will speak of my own accountability when it comes to understanding that Palestinians have been experiencing this for much longer than we, the world, have been watching this year. However, there is no denying that this year brought things that we cannot fathom. Horrors unimaginable across our screens. Yesterday I wept at various times throughout the day. My nervous system frayed from completing the manuscript review of this book, from remembering the early parts of this past year, and all that I witnessed, and from knowing it's not only ongoing, but that Israel in recent weeks has invaded Lebanon, and that more people, children, families, bloodlines, are experiencing even more extreme suffering than before I wrote this book.

And yet, I believe in the power of words. I believe in the power of this book to continue to change culture. I told my generous and faithful editor, Jazz Cook, "I want to ensure that for any event I do, anywhere, for as long as I am alive, that this book will be on the merch table." It's a small act in some ways, and yet in this world that has censored the artists and the poets, that has tried to silence us through means of propaganda, bullying and lies, I must believe it matters. Thank you, dear one, for picking up these pages. For honouring this witnessing, for giving these poems, these stories, your time.

To Palestinians,

I begin with an apology. To Lebanese people, to Iraqi and Irani and Syrian and Congolese and Sudanese people, I am sorry. I am sorry that it took me until October 2023 to open my eyes and learn more about what has been happening to your people, your homelands, your children. I am sorry, and I am grateful to you for your grace and friendship, and for the ways your courage lights a fire in me to never be silent in the face of injustice. Thank you for waking us up. Thank you for your dedication. Thank you for relentlessly speaking up loud enough that I finally heard. May more of us awaken. May more of us listen.

Following this apology, it is important to me to give you more context. Hu nini Ktunaxa. *I am Ktunaxa.* I am a member of a First Nation in so-called Canada, and for Ktunaxa, there are no words in our language to say, "I'm sorry." Instead, when we asked our Elders if we had a Ktunaxa concept for the English word "reconciliation," there was silence. For Ktunaxa, when our Elders are silent, they may be thinking hard about an answer, or they may be signalling that we are asking the wrong kind of question.

As we pressed on, asking about how people acknowledged harm, it became clear that for Ktunaxa, a high-context culture, we couldn't speak about a general harm, but had to talk about what brought us "out of balance" in the first place. It became clear that to absolve ourselves of harm, we must be accountable through our *actions*. In a Ktunaxa understanding, we must work to bring things back into balance, and in doing so correct the harm we've caused. In order to "fix our road," as we say, we must do something differently than we did when we caused the harm.

This book is a beginning, a continuing and a seed for the future. This book is an offering of amends through action. What I have heard most from Palestinians since October 2023 is the call to speak up. This book is my initial attempt at answering that call. On October 18th,

2023, after witnessing eleven days of escalation of Palestinian genocide following the events of October 7th, I posted the first poem in this book on Instagram. In witnessing the horrors—of children being pulled out from under the rubble of their homes, of bombs dropping on tents, of consistent removal, packing few belongings and being forced into travel, people becoming refugees in seconds, told to evacuate to safe zones that never ended up being safe—I was called to return to a practice of poetry. In times like these, the role of the poet becomes less muddy for me. When Palestinian poets are being targeted and murdered for their words, it becomes my responsibility, as a poet, to find my own words, to practice our art, to help readers and audiences make connections they may otherwise not see in this world.

Poetry has always been an experience of connection for me. It is important to me to connect to my audience. In these poems, it is my hope that I am helping you make connections. Connections between those of us watching as we experience this devastation from the strange place of comfort and privilege across the world, and connections with Palestinians, calling out over the internet for us to witness, to speak, to say their names and tell their stories, and see the connections between genocides—between what has happened to my people here and what is happening to your people over there. Connections between the stories and the lives and the deaths of our families, communities and children.

I am sorry I didn't commit to learning about Palestine before. I commit and recommit to learning, listening, and when called to, speaking—as often and as loud as I can—since understanding what I have been witnessing over the last year.

On Apology

I open this preface with an apology because I now realize that I am sorry I didn't try harder before fall of 2023. I am sorry that I took the "complexities" of the Palestine/Israel "conflict" at face value. That even while being steeped in critical thought about colonialism in my own Ktunaxa context, I was unable to see the similarities until they were right in front of me; a colonial genocide being livestreamed on my cell phone, through Instagram, an app I had downloaded years before to share photos of my friends at parties and the meals we ate.

There are no words to signal apology in the Ktunaxa language. This strikes me as important in our context; in this country they call Canada, during this time that we often call the "Age of Reconciliation." In 2008, then Prime Minister Stephen Harper issued "a Statement of Apology to former students of Indian Residential Schools."[1] At the time, my grandma attended a gathering of residential school survivors to hear this statement. She also went through the process of sharing her stories, only to have lawyers tell her which ones were "provable" (the ones she, at 70+ years old, still had physical scars from) and which ones were not (the ones that left invisible fears, palpable only inside her, but not enough for the "justice system" in Canada to see.) As much as I can critique these moments, I know that all of this meant something to her. I know it means something to me too.

I know some of my readers will be wondering why I am speaking all this in a book for Palestine. First, I imagine some of you don't have a history of who I am, as a Ktunaxa person. I am from a people who pre-date the country they call Canada by tens of thousands of years, or, as my teachers say, "we've been here since the animals were the people." We are told that we are the blood of a being who was killed during the formation of the Rocky Mountains. We are only now, over 150 years since the confederation of a foreign government on our (Indigenous) lands, beginning to understand the weight of what has happened to our people.

Palestine is bringing that clarity for me. There is a weight to understanding a colonial government is starving people in the same way they did to our own ancestors. I keep seeing an image, referenced in poem "76," of the Royal Canadian Mounted Police (RCMP) breaking into Unist'ot'en Camp tearing down a barricade set up by land and water protectors, cutting through a sign that says "reconciliation"[2] before arresting matriarchs and grandmothers as they sang prayer songs. I am now aware that many of the RCMP in Canada have trained with the Israel Occupation Force (IOF).[3] Colonialism is interconnected in so many of the ways we (Indigenous peoples) understand interconnection. Just as biodiversity is reliant on these connections, the destruction of life finds its way around the world in similar ways.

Statement of Reconciliation

To return to the voices of our Ktunaxa Elders, I share with you that upon further discussion, and when we explained the context of why we wanted to hear about "reconciliation" (that we were asking about this concept in terms of Indian Residential schools) they came up with the following statement, which is republished in poem "20." This statement took many meetings, and was finalized by the Ktunaxa Nation Council's Traditional Knowledge and Language Advisory Committee on August 16, 2018:

nini ku qaɬwiynaɬa

[this is what is in our hearts]

qaqaʔni ma yaqawitknawaski

[what they did to us is true]

q̇apiɬpaɬnin

[say it all/tell the whole story]

mika yaqaɬitknawaski hu qayaqaɬqa¢aɬani

[despite what happened to us we made it through]

hu qaɬwinaɬani ku¢ sukiɬ ʔaqsɬmaknik naɬa

[we want a good life for ourselves]

hawi¢kinin k¢mak kyam ¢ ¢ina·kinin

[hold the truth and go forward].

¢inɬ qaqa

[so be it]

maʔ¢ kuktkinin!

[do not change this statement!][4]

When I teach about this statement, I talk about how much we can learn from these words. That first line, "*this is what is in our hearts*"; our hearts are where Ktunaxa find knowing. This reference to our hearts is a reference to the deep knowledges that we have carried forward through generations. This is followed by an assertion of truth. Still today we see residential school denialism among Canadians just as we see our leaders debating terms of "genocide" when it comes to Palestine. How many resources are used for this debate that could be used to end the genocide, instead?

This third statement, "q̓apiⱡpaⱡnin" or "*say it all/tell the whole story*," is a call that I am answering with this book. While I am unable to tell the entire story of what is happening in Palestine, or even of what has happened to us, as Ktunaxa in so-called Canada, I am answering the call of Palestinians and my Ktunaxa Elders alike: to speak. To share the stories of lives lost, of trauma inflicted upon us, of what it means to survive a genocide.

It is my prayer that years from now Palestinians will be able to echo the words of Ktunaxa here "*despite what happened to us we made it through*." I refuse to imagine a world without Palestinians. Just as there is no word in Ktunaxa for "I'm sorry," there is no word in our language for "extinct." May we honour this knowledge and continue to pray, fight for, and honour Palestinian life and Indigenous futures.

When I hear the fourth statement, I cannot help but think of the Palestinian people I have witnessed celebrating children's birthdays, dancing dabke, delighting at finding a blooming poppy or a small turtle, flying kites made of the limited emergency supplies they have amongst the devastation of the genocide they are living through.

We want a good life for ourselves.

There are a thousand and one stories by racists and colonizers about what Indigenous people want. I have heard it all. And yet, I remember these words from my knowledge holders. I remember the words of Palestinian poets and writers and young people who have had to become journalists out of necessity, not out of a dream. They want to return. They want to inhabit their homes and go to their schools and drink their teas and nourish themselves with the foods and waters of their homelands. They want to grow the olive trees of their ancestors and watch sunrises and sunsets in peace in their homelands.

We want a good life for ourselves.

I have recently read a horrifying statistic from 2021 that the average life expectancy for a First Nations man living in Alberta has dropped to 60 years old (nearly 20 years lower than the average non-First Nations man).[5] When my Elders share this statement, we are saying: we want our children to live long, happy and healthy lives.

I extend that to Palestinian children and their families; parents, grandparents, siblings, cousins, aunties, uncles, community members, school teachers. No person should go through what Palestinians are facing now. No Ktunaxa person should have gone through what my ancestors went through either.

There's a saying in our Ktunaxa culture that we each walk our own road. When someone is straying off their path, or taking a side route, we may hear a call from our aunties or family members to "fix" our "road." I think of this when I think of the concept of apology. Perhaps I was on the wrong road for a bit, so what do I need to fix it? Sometimes I've gone far down that wrong road and need to backtrack some miles before being able to find my way. Other days, I may have only taken a step or two and can easily correct my actions.

Palestine, this book is the beginning of "fixing my road." I will admit, as a young Indigenous person growing up in ʔamakʔis Ktunaxa (small-town southeastern British Columbia, Canada), I did not know about your people or what was happening in your lands.

Seeds

It has become important for me to share my journey to shouting "Free Palestine!" loud and clear and without shame or fear. We know that there are still many people who don't understand, who have chosen to look away, or who feel like it's all just too much to understand. Perhaps they do understand, but fear speaking up. Perhaps the cost feels too high. This next section outlines a bit of my history, to offer up that each time we think of Palestine, and each time we are brought into interacting with Palestinian stories, I believe a seed is planted. While none of these things got me as far as this year has, these are moments on my road when I could not look away. I think they are also important to remember, to honour the work of all the incredible thinkers, knowledge holders, speakers, intellectuals, artists and activists who were doing this work long before I began writing poems.

When I went away to Simon Fraser University (named after a colonizer of Coast Salish Lands) I began to connect with larger communities, most specifically LGBTQ+ people, and I vaguely remember conversations of pinkwashing happening at that time. I will admit I didn't look far into the conversation. I was afraid of my own queerness and was overwhelmed by the journey I was on—of learning the truths about what had happened to my own people. I want it to be clear here that my own Two Spirit identity, my identity as a transgender person and my identity as a queer man, only serve to deepen my desire to speak up for Palestine. While this initial moment interacting with these ideas didn't immediately get me here, it was a moment on my road that led me to today's commitment. I will not allow pinkwashing to sway me.

The next thing I can remember in my work of fixing my road was when the Indigenous academic community expressed outrage at the un-hiring "controversy" involving Palestinian and Jordanian professor Steven Salaita in the 2010s.[6] I wore a pin a friend gifted me that said "Fuck Civility," and yet, I didn't fully comprehend what was happening outside of my belief in academic freedoms and the deep feeling of knowing when an injustice had happened.

It was a few years later (years in which I enrolled in a PhD program, moved across the country, got sober, came out as transgender and began participating in Indigenous ceremony) that I found myself on Facebook sharing about how happy I was with my switch from sugary sodas to carbonated water because I had bought a Soda Stream. I am grateful now to the Indigenous Studies professor who brought my attention to the company being Israeli owned. While there is a pang of shame, I share this story to honour those who are coming to this fight late (all of us), and who may relate to this consistent unknowing. I had seen the proud stamp of "Made in Israel" on the box but had not understood, at the time, what the BDS (Boycott, Divest and Sanction) movement was, or how it applied to this company. That being said, a few days after the post and comment, I felt a familiar nagging, like something just wasn't sitting right with me about the whole thing. I posted a request to my Facebook friends and followers on November 9, 2017:

> So, insecure truth-telling time: I know very little about Israel/Palestine conflicts, and what I can do to (help? ...probably the wrong word) context: I'm trying to learn about BDS due to my previous Soda Stream post and it's become very clear to me that I know very little about the complexities of this situation-which is probably why I haven't tried to learn anything before now...
>
> My truth is that I work where my gifts are used best: at home, in our Indigenous communities, with Indigenous students, and in the Canadian/Indigenous context that I have spent the last 10 years of post-secondary learning about.
>
> That being said, I don't believe that we exist in a vacuum, and I think it's time for me to open my eyes a bit.
>
> It's going to have to stay on the corner of my desk, but if there are folks that know more about this and are willing to say, grab a coffee, set a time to skype chat, or whatever (fully out

of interest/passions sake, and in full recognition that I am requesting some labour from you) I would be grateful and I think we could have some good conversations, because I think there are connections to be made.

Also, if you've got books/articles etc. out there to recommend, I'll add them to the list. Because I recognize there are many scholars and folks who have done the work to make the connections that I "think there are" to be had, already. Due to current time constraints (ie. writing my own dissertation) I simply spend time searching on my own right now, but please trust I will do the labour of reading whatever you do the labour of sending my way.

As always, your support in my learning endeavours is greatly appreciated.

In many Indigenous cultures, including Ktunaxa, the number seven holds spiritual significance. I have learned that in seven years, much can change. It's not lost on me that I will be completing final edits on this book going to production around the same time that seven years has passed since this initial post. While I admit my first round of research from this initial post was lacking, I want to be clear that it's because the propaganda and desire for me not to know is so strong in the world. I remember reading links and finding so much about the "complexity" of the "conflict." I remember feeling confused, and instead of pushing through that confusion, stepping away, returning to learning about contexts I understood more easily, and to my own little life. It's so easy in this capitalist world to look away.

And yet, I know that post planted a seed. The story of Steven Salaita cultivated the earth for this seed. Rectifying my limited understanding of pinkwashing shook loose what I understood about the world and made way for my commitment to writing and publishing this collection.

I have been asked what made me start, and again, with my neurodivergent trauma brain, I'm not sure exactly what image it was that pulled me to write. When I teach creative writing workshops, I often say "I am a poet because when the feeling gets too big, I need somewhere to put it." What I can say is that the feelings witnessing the initial days of this present-day Palestinian genocide were far too much for me to contain within myself.

I saw children with their limbs blown off, I saw entire blocks of housing brought down to rubble, I saw hundreds of Palestinians walking through the streets in terror, trying to help each other, trying to find where the calls of pain were coming from underneath the rubble of their homes. I witnessed surgeons performing surgery on people with no anesthetic. I became familiar with the names of Palestinian youth-become-journalists; Bisan Owda (@wizard_bisan1), Motaz Azaiza (@motaz_azaiza), Plestia Alaqad (@plestia.alaqad), and those of the diaspora, like Jenan Matari (@jenanmatari) and Tasha Nadia Matar (@tahrirtherapy). I connected with acquaintances, some I had only met in person briefly, others I had only met on zoom, who were following, sharing, posting and witnessing alongside me. At some point, I started referring to these relationships as "comrades in genocide." After the first poem, there came another and another.

At some point I realized that this genocide would be ongoing. At some point, in spite of my desire and hope for a heroic stop to the violence, in spite of my faltering faith in the systems, I began faxing each poem to the office of Justin Trudeau. I wrote my local Conservative MP, and had a racist diatribe emailed back to me. I donated to GoFundMes and raffles, I joined local groups and signed on to speak at panels in other cities, months down the road, because I learned that this was not going to be an easy ending. I learned that I would need to sustain. I kept writing poems.

Perhaps two or three months in, I realized that this sustained practice would go on longer than anticipated. I realized that while the swell of pro-Palestinian protests and phone calls to our government gave me the hope that this would end quickly—that our governments would listen to us, the people, and stop these horrors from happening—my hope and this fire inside me wasn't enough to stop colonization across the world. I kept writing poems, and slowly my goal became to reach one hundred poems. This book, *Born Sacred: Poems for Palestine*, holds those one hundred poems, which I wrote between October 2023 and April 2024, as I worked through all the feelings that came along with being a survivor of genocide, while witnessing genocide happening in real time across the world from me.

I refuse any ambiguity. My heart and spirit stand for a free Palestine. These poems are one small act of resistance. One small act of "fixing my road," and committing myself to the truth that I have stepped into in witnessing and speaking out for Palestinian life. I hope it blossoms a seed of resilience in you too.

On a final note, I want to share that this book would not be possible without Black activists. I would not have awoken so abruptly to Palestine if I had not been awakened by Black Lives Matter, to concepts like reparations and abolitionism. I would not be here to write these poems without so many incredible Indigenous people before me. In the initial draft of this preface, I had proposed republishing work from the late Sto:lo aunty, Lee Maracle, however, I instead want to direct you, reader, to her entire book, *Talking to the Diaspora*, inscribed "for Mahmoud Darwish & the children of Gaza."[7]

I am far from the first Indigenous person in Canada to understand and draw attention to the connections between our people and the people of Palestine. May this book inspire others, and may we continue writing, fighting, resisting, loving, breathing and connecting until we see our dream of a Free Palestine, and #landback throughout the world, come true.

— **SMOKII SUMAC**, October 2024

1.

today
my body is in pain
every piece of wood
i stacked to get ready
for winter
for winter

for my love to
keep the home fire
burning

every movement
etched into my
muscles
every time
i laid another piece
on the wood pile
i said a prayer

no more war
help us all
find the peace
of stacking
wood
for winter

may the fires of Palestine
turn to those of warming
peace

a cats head resting
beside them

may the burning of
bomb explosions
cease

and the fires
of nourishment and
rest be lit

freedom
to stack wood

to prepare for
a future
we can
trust
will
come

2.

i pour water for my tea

> *i lost my water ration for
> the day*

my husband waters the
plants

> *500mL
> the water has been cut off*

i let the water pour over
me in the shower
longer than usual
today

> *the women are taking
> pills
> to stop menstruation
> no water to clean*

i fill up the water glass
beside my bed

> *i lost my water ration for
> the day*

i pour fresh water
into the cup
on my altar

    and
    pray
    for
    Palestine

> *free
> free
> Palestine*

3.

today i woke up
sobbing

a truth screaming
into my being

from my unconscious
from the place
truth lives

when we wont
look at it

        how do so many
           look away?

      soothe themselves
        tell each other
          little stories

        close their eyes
          drive away

         how do we
           go on?

                 today i woke up
                   sobbing
                i watched a video
           of a Palestinian child
       crying for their mother

           felt the deep well of pain
           inside me
           remembering crying
           for my own

                 how many generations
                  taught not to cry?
                    to take it out
                    on themselves?

           the least i can do
           is weep today
                 let the truth
                break me open

4.

our Ktunaxa nation
went to
the supreme court
to fight for
our sacred
places

all places are sacred

the court
said our name wrong
told us
our religion
has no space here

the developer of
the proposed ski resort
said
he wouldnt call
that place
sacred

all places are sacred

yesterday
they bombed
a church
in Palestine

a church
that was older
than the state
of israel

and i think of how
when notre dame burned
financially wealthy
white people
sent millions

what of that
which is sacred
to us?

all places
all people
all children
born sacred

5.

i will kiss you in heaven[8]

my husband
waving at me
blowing a kiss
as he leaves for the
weekend

to visit an old friend

the thought crosses my
mind
he reminds me of
an old movie

anticipatory grief
they call it

an old vhs tape
an image i will hold
in my mind
for years
to come

when we know the one
we love
is going to pass

sometimes in these
moments
i feel it already

blowing a kiss
telling us he loves us
me
the dog
our house

and then
my weeping
begins
again

as i think of every
unsent
kiss
goodbye
from the hands
and lips
in Palestine
in israel
here in north america
where new death
is reported
every
day

6.

the words come
slower today
and still
i must write this poem

drank two cups of
coffee
yesterday
panic
attack
day

got another email   *they dropped bombs*
about a work   *all night*
situation   *canada*
                                                  made a statement
                                                  supporting israel
panic
attack   *saskatchewan*
day   *used the notwithstanding*
                                      clause (unrelated but so
                                      related)
took a little drive
walked by the river   the news
                                                      the news

my love   my love
came home   came home
safe   safe

and i wept
as he held me
and when i woke
in the middle of the night
it was peaceful
warm
quiet in the dark

                    as the bombs
                  dropped all night
                        across
                      the world

7.

i keep waking up
in the middle of the night
last night
the inconvenience
getting to me

i take iron pills
these days
and they make me
nauseous

again
an
inconvenience

the inconvenience
of cancelling streaming
services

of going without
my favourite warm
fall
drink

what is an
inconvenience
worth?

sometimes to the ones
we love
that small sacrifice
can light up the world

sometimes when you
hear a three year old
gave up her disney
subscription
you remember

seven generations

none of us free
until all of us free

the inconvenience
of knowing
this world isnt safe
for all of us

a poem
a prayer
each day
its own
small sacrifice
let it add up
let it
take a bite out of this
thing
this capitalist
war
machine

let us be
inconvenienced

8.

the last therapist
michael
was big on internal
family
systems

as i am convening
with my inner
children

one of them
comes
screaming forward

was i eleven?
twelve?

                  every remembrance day
                  marked by
                  poems
                  poppies
                  a school play

                          think of all the kids
                        wearing orange shirts
                        decades since i was
                                    their age

                  my inner preteen
                  cant stop screaming

                        we were taught
                      the wars had ended
                      we were taught
                      Never Again

                and in Palestine

                      the children
                      the children

9.

blank page
blank mind

you called to check on
a friend yesterday

shes had covid
and you remember
how it felt

not sure if youd
survive
              keep writing
she told you

                    the compounding losses
connecting over   have me considering
being artists   what it means to
in a time of war   have faith in the
                    next life
                          may the spirits of
                       Palestinian children
                                rest

                        may they return
                            renewed
                     in a world changed
                         by them

                 a bird
             hit my window
               yesterday
         i held my breath and
                prayed
      anticipating the worst
             and then
           tears of relief
         as they flew away
        to live another day

10.

things that have
brought me hope

after Salma
talks about
Palestinians
living outside
of capitalism—

        sharing bread
        taking care of
            each
            other

                            this morning
        barefoot   i read about pluto
      in the rubble   the planet of death
      still rushing   and rebirth
         to help

                    takes centuries to circle

—i begin ruminating
on hope
                    pluto in scorpio—
        hope is not linear   *—this generation possesses*
        healing is not linear   *the abilities to initiate*
                    change on a world-wide
                    basis…they may
                    experience conflict on a
                    world-wide basis. They will
                    be forced to learn the right
                    use of the world's
                    resources.[9]
        reminds me of the
        eighth fire

        reminds me
        the fall of systems
        that harm us

                    will not come
                      easy

hope is not linear

who would hope for
this
collapse?

knowing the toll
it is taking

and yet
there is hope
in the responses
of those
continuing to sing
continuing to hold
the deepest wells
of compassion
for each other

as everything private
becomes public

as mourning
becomes so far
reaching so
collective

hope sparks
and flames
and flickers in
this night

11.

full moon
lunar eclipse

    we dont recommend
            rituals
    during the eclipse

the lights
go out
    the lights
    went out
the light
feels
out

    unpredictable
    unharnessable
    unwitnessed

forget what they say
    we pray

ritual and prayer
keeping the connection

    keep praying
    keep going
    keep doing
    keep talking

the lights
the water
the internet
the supplies
the food
the food!
the ceiling
the buildings
the air
the air
the air

white
phosphorous
and death

the lights
went out
in Palestine

they do not want us
to see

12.

Anishinaabeg stand with Palestine

a found poem from @raunchykwe's speech posted October 26, 2023, that was spoken at a protest against genocide, in support of Palestinian people in Anishinaabeg territories.[10]

stand with
grapple with   this country
the removal   is founded
of Indigenous bodies   on genocide

                                                the state
unthinkable   every   attempts to
harm   part   destroy
flooding our   body   life
homelands   being
                         ancestors
                         stand with
                         Palestine

                    keep coming back

purpose   the only way forward
love and meaning   no liberation
sense of security   without
witnessing   Palestine
society
my daughter

                                 what could be more important?

                    i refuse   experiences of
             to let my daughter   settler colonialism
             inherit a world   intertwined
                build from   structures of
                genocide   empire

                                     free Palestine
                                     humanity
                                     free Palestine

13.

at some point
i start to feel panicked
angry
lashing out
unfollowing those
who i dont see posting

grief draws a line

wisdom from a mother
who knows that grief
intimately

when our warrior mom
went starside
i called the people
who knew grief
well

a reflection stays with me

when youre okay
let yourself be
the grief will return
hold the refrain

yesterday i logged on
to a prayer gathering
three or four screens
of faces and names

as we held space
in deep prayer
in deep grief

i wept openly
my body releasing
all that i am holding

those leading us
the healers who
opened up this space

asked us to call upon
our most healed
grandmothers

there is something in this—

                              —recognizing our ancestors
                                on their own healing roads

there is privilege and power
                              in healing

yesterday i remembered the teaching

            the
                        practice
we must beg
                        we must call out to them
                        like in ceremony

and i see that
                        for those of us

allowing Gaza to
                        wake us
grief is
                        changing us
let us
              all
                        be changed

                              from river
                                to sea

14.

yesterday
on a zoom call
they asked me about
my experience
with translating
my poem

there are hierarchies
of grief
into Ktunaxa
the language
of my ancestors

in our language
they say

i spoke of how
both my grandmothers
had passed
my aunty too
and i believed
i would never
learn

theres no word for
extinct

today there is a
version of that poem
in my voice
in our language

i have no Ktunaxa elders
i used to say

feel the deep well
in my chest
to think of what this
means

grief
for all the ways
genocide
has stolen
from me

there are languages
traditions
customs and culture
the ways we greet
each other
the ways we mourn
there are works of art
to be made
songs to be sung
bread to be kneaded
in just the
way
the aunties
and grandmothers
taught
there are aunties
and grandmothers and
fathers and
families to visit with
in Palestine

free them all
their great great grandchildren
need them
here

15.

it wasnt until
university
i learned of what
they call
      the trail of tears

the Cherokee Removal
they call it
and Choctaw and
Muskogee (Creek)
and Seminole
and
and
and
      a forced march
      from their homelands
      the military
      walking some
      sixteen
      thousand
      Indigenous bodies
      to the newly formed
      "Indian territory" of
      oklahoma
      (which of course
      did not remain
      Indian territory)

i am no authority on this
      story
i only know what ive
      been taught

we know the stories
of too many deaths
      on that road
we know
these stories

yet they ban telling them
in schools now

      and in Palestine
i start to have a knowing

      they are
mass murdering
so those left
will be easier
to remove

they are attempting to
erase an entire
people

      because they
      want the land

        an old story
        a new story

            these spirits
          who only know
           how to take

                    it is said
                    the people sang
                    on the trail of tears
                    songs still sung
                    in ceremonies
                    across the land

                            sing a prayer song
                              for Palestine
                            pray the songs
                            will continue
                                  being
                                  sung

16.

he called for a
"pause"

as those direct
actions
interrupted
his speech

as i was drafting
this poem
in my head

(been up for hours)

i considered calling him
the most powerful man
in the world

what is power?

                        it is said we once respected
                        our enemies so much that
                        we would consume a part
                        of them to embody their
                                warrior spirit

                                what then
                                with enemies
                        i cannot find respect for?

on that other platform
the one for the "old people"
a Jewish friend

one that mere years ago
made matzah ball soup
for the first ancestors
feast
that i held

we shared stories   *what is power?*
of grandmothers
ancestors   the power of cyclists
food   bringing bread to the
tradition   people

he made his profile   the power of Jewish
picture say   comrades
ceasefire now   being arrested
and the commenters   in nyc
went wild

the power of
it strikes me   prayer song
then how much pain   of witnessing
they are in   of doing
i can hold space   something
for your pain   anything
i type back

let that man with authority
find his real power
now

may we find a way
to hold each other in all our
unending pain

none of us free
until all of us are

39

17.

two days ago
my husband and i
carpooled in
dropped off the dog
at his playcare
went to the nation clinic
got our
new vaccines
and flu shots

        he works with kids
sneezing on him all the
           time
       i get on planes
where nobody wears a
          mask
yet we get this protection
         easily
healthcare ready and
      waiting for us

yesterday
it snowed
a soft blanket of
quiet white flakes
covering
everything

      we decided to
    work from home
     even take an
       afternoon
         nap

all day
as i feel the quiet
of this home near the woods

the quiet of the snow fall
the quiet of the dark
this morning

i think of the research
on sound and our
nervous systems

i weep openly
remembering Palestine
trying to send some
semblance of this quiet
to the children
who cannot sleep

to the mothers
who cannot comfort
the fathers and uncles and
brothers searching for water and
bread
searching for the bodies of
loved ones

when will they know
quiet?

                              how many years from now
                              will the sound of a plane
                                    terrorize them?

            the bombs   the bombs

                              the screaming

            i have been around
                              death
            i can understand
                              the weight
            of the moment
                              a soul
            leaves
                              a body
            this is too many
            the constant
            noise of it
            the only   quiet
                                          here
                        on the other side
                              of the world
            i pray for quiet
            for the people   not in death
                              but in peace

                        end the occupation
                              bring quiet
                              to Palestine
                              the people
                              need
                              quiet

18.

*we could
be free
right
now*

the people have
forgotten
vengeance
in the ways we
knew
before

         revenge has become
         an ugly thing
         inflated by the greed
         of corporations
         and men

there are old stories
of the things that
lived under the ice
under the ground
buried
way down deep
somewhere it cant hurt anyone else

         we talked to the elders
         about a place
         that we knew
         wasnt safe

         yet they dug and dug
         into these
         burial grounds

         of course
         they settled there
         anyways
         and then the mountain
         moved

         qakiɫiɫni
         they were told

         qa ȼinkapaɫtiɫik
         they just didnt listen

the people have
forgotten
how to
listen
                              pride
                thick and sticky
                  filling their
                          ears
                         eyes
                       mouths
they called us
savages
                                              in the old way
                                              we took a life
              yet never questioned   for a life
                     each other   but only if we
                                                            had to
in the old way   in the old way
there were   vengeance
roles   meant taking in
                     there were people   the families of those
                   who came earthside   gone
                     with a purpose—   to become your
                      to take care of   own
                        those things   even
                                           those of your
                                                          enemy
                                           a balancing

                                                   a rebalancing

                                           the teachings of the intricate
                                           nature of balance
                                           tell us

                                              a reckoning
                                              a balancing

                                                  will come

                                           are you listening?

19.

every morning
my heart goes
immediately
to Palestine

last night
we feasted
the ancestors

and this morning
one of the first stories
i see
is an all
too
familiar one—

do you see what theyre
letting in?

its shrouds to cover
our deceased

they are sending
good quality shrouds
for us

good cotton brand
in huge quantities

—no food
no water
no medicine

in 2009 when our people
were dying of swine flu
the canadian government
sent body bags

in 2020
native american health
centers asked for covid 19
supplies and the
us government
sent body bags

i tell my therapist
yes we survived genocide
but not like that

active
war
zone

my therapist
reminds me
comparison
doesnt make sense
in this context

we know these stories
intimately
in our bodies

yesterday
millions marched
here in canada
and the united
states

                    the family group chat

                    went to a march with 300 000 people

        an anti genocide march?

                    yeah

                good
        im proud of you

                    and i see jingle dancers
                    and i see monique and quill
                    aruna and surya

        these are my people
        they are all our people
                Palestinians

                    our people

        and i see that when the
        police stopped our people

                    from going any further
                    they all kneeled down
                    bowed their heads
                    to pray

                send them
                medicine
                send them
                    water
                supply
                the living

                    no more martyrs
                    their blood is on
                            your hands

20.

Keep my stories alive so you
keep me alive. Remember that
I wanted a normal life, a small
home full of my children's laughter
and the smell of my wife's cooking.
Remember that the world that
pretended to be the saviour of
humanity participated in killing
such a small dream. —Tareq
Hajjaj, a journalist and writer[11]

ṅini ku kaɫwiynaɫa
this is whats in our hearts

qaqaʔni ma yaqaɫitknawaski
what they did to us is true

qapiɫpaɫnin
say it all/tell the whole story

Keep my stories alive so you
keep me alive. Remember that
I wanted a normal life, a small
home full of my children's laughter
and the smell of my wife's cooking.
Remember that the world that
pretended to be the saviour of
humanity participated in killing
such a small dream. —Tareq
Hajjaj, a journalist and writer

mika yaqaɫitknawaski hu
qayaqaɫqaȼaɫani
despite what happened to us
we made it through

hu qaɫwinaɫani kuȼ sukiɫ
ʔaqɫmakṅik̓ naɫa
we want a good life for ourselves

Keep my stories alive so you
keep me alive. Remember that
I wanted a normal life, a small
home full of my children's laughter
and the smell of my wife's cooking.
Remember that the world that
pretended to be the saviour of
humanity participated in killing
such a small dream. —Tareq
Hajjaj, a journalist and writer

hawiȼkinin kȼmak̓ kyam ȼ
ȼina·kinin
hold the truth and go forward

ȼinɫ qaqa
so be it

maʔȼ kuktkinin!
do not change this statement![12]

21.

days ago i wrote
about my rage

                                     unfollowing people
                                        feeling my heart
                                                    cut ties

a message came in then
reminding me

                                     gaining new friends
                                     and comrades too
                                          though

when our mom
was alive
i remember her
talking about
how there were

                    trump signs
                        in one yard   *Black Lives Matter*
                                              signs
                                              in another

remember her reflecting
on whether she—the lightest
skinned of us—

                              —should start answering
                                        the door

        i think of that fear
    of the "games" the rez kids know
              too well
              hiding
      when there was a knock
          at the door
        (oh you didnt play
            that game?)

                          i think of how back home
                              in this territory
                            we build houses
                            over our lodges
                          so nobody can see

                          remnants of a history
                        where we were persecuted
                          for being ourselves

they dont feel like remnants
anymore

as the gulf between
those who still look away
and the rest of us
widens

and so
i pray
in the ways
i know how
and i share
those ways
as best
i can
and i hear
the haunting words

i will never forget

those who kept going
those who protected
their own "mental health"

because when it comes
down to it
it tells me
they will be clinking their
glasses
going on their vacations
even if it was me
even when it was

may we all find the friends
the comrades
who will stand beside us
as the revolution
comes

22.

one month
thirty days
over
ten
thousand
martyrs

        yesterday
        i picked up
         a small
      anniversary gift

        our wedding
          was four
           months
             ago
when i teach
about
ndn time
i teach that
time isnt real   how can i teach that
that   today?
        everything
         happens   nothing is as its
  when its supposed to   supposed to be

                 thirty days
                 of bombing
                 one month
                 centuries
                 seventy
                 five
                 years

               what is a day
               to a mother
           whispering goodbye
            to her child?

today is
aboriginal
veterans day

i was taught
to respect
those who
went to war

i was taught
we were
peace
keepers

                          remember
                      before our flag
                      meant freedom
                       (the kind that
                      tortures you by
                       honking and
                           partying
                       in your city?)

everything
i have been
taught
about freedom
about
this
war machine

                          now buried
                     under the rubble
                        in Palestine

23.

in the dark of this
almost winter morning
i feel as though
i am out of words

i go search the news
read the gaslighting
media with theyre
meaningless statements

*"involving several people
who align with opposing
sides"*

the acrobatics
they have to do
to avoid
being anti genocide
abhorrent

and then a headline
catches my eye
my heart
the pit of my stomach
trigger
warning
this whole fucking world
needs a god damn
warning

when i was teaching at
universities
indigenous studies

i would teach
about oka
i would say things like

*if these ancestors were
yours would you want
them disturbed? would
white settlers do this to
their dead?*

today we have been
seeing bodies in shrouds for
more than a month in
Palestine—the haunting
images the feelings i have
for families who cannot
honour and grieve their
dead

and in colorado
oh i dont even want to
write it
i dont want to know
this

this morning
i read about
a funeral home
in colorado
where
nearly
two hundred
loved ones
were never
cremated   families

sent ashes
of who knows
what
while their
loved ones
were hidden
in a warehouse
for years

my heart oh my heart
as i realize that so many
dont care about these
images we are seeing
because they are blinded
they do this to their own
they put profit over
people

theyve
forgotten
how to
honour
the dead

24.

this grief makes our
bodies sick for
generations

life expectancy
lowered

nervous systems
wired for
entire
lives

                every
           meeting with
            our elders
         used to end in
                yelling

            my uncle
            did work
        teaching them

collective trauma
                                        what we are seeing
                                        reverberates out
                                        into the future
                                        in ways that are
                                        unfathomable
                                        unimaginable

                                  a hundred years from now
                                      a descendant
                                    of the Palestinians
                                      we see here

                                      raises their voice
                                      at their partner

                                          pain
                                        echoes
                                        forward

let there be joy
remembered
in their bodies
too

Plestia
and an old woman
smiling at a
tiny turtle

children singing
a song to
celebrate
a birthday
amidst the rubble

the smile on the
birthday childs face
palpable

a new memory
amongst the constant
sound of the bombs

let them remember the day it
finally ended
let it come in their
lifetimes
before they die
before they grow old

before
tomorrow

25.

today i write my name
on
my hand

we are waiting for
martyrdom at
any
moment

today i write my name
on
my hand
        there are only
        children
        left

       we bid farewell to the
       children
      left them on machines
      under the threat
      of weapons

                                i think of writing some
      no one is at the   comparison
      hospital
      but them   yesterday i forgot the
                      shopping list at home
                      and in Palestine
                             Osama
                          writes his name
                           on his hand

                        to be remembered

           to be remembered

                        what is this life?
                  where my days go on
                  and the children
                     the children
                      left alone
                   in a hospital
                     to die

a year or so ago

        in one of my
        depressions

i watched this show
about a hospital
in new orleans
          during
          and after
the hurricane—
      —a true story

apparently
the nurses
helped people
die   euthanized
            them
because they
        couldnt

get them   for the first time
       to safety   i consider

                     the ethics of that
                     in a new light

                 an unfathomable
                 choice

                 and i pray
                      for Osama

                 i pray for
                     the children

                   i

                      pray

26.

there is a teaching
that was offered to me

         and so
         i offer it
         to you

this teaching
is about those moments
when we see an animal
pass   —like a bird

         hitting a window—

       that we pray for it to
           come again
             quickly
          into a new life

                i was taught to
              face them south
            to help with that
                 transition

as we watch
so many
new lives
return starside
so quick   so many
            babies
             and
        young ones

i find myself
wrestling with
this teaching   this context
              seems so far
           from the bird
           the window
             the deer
             on the road

my prayer has shifted
        may they stay
         in the stars
       as long as they
           need to

        i pray that
        by the time they come back
        their memories will have
        helped us change this world
        so they can have peace upon
        their
                    return

27.

the time is
now
the place is
here
     a song i have sung
     a thousand times

a bank
funding
israeli arms
also funds
the arts
     i dont look up
     what the bank
     funding the project
     i am working on
     has done—

          —i already know

gratitude for those
who stood up
to say *end the genocide*
last night
at the awards
ceremony
               yesterday
            for the first time
              i was asked
            to be on camera
               in the uber

                 at first
            i felt concerned
               is it because
             i look native
          is it because of the
              blue hair

and then i listened to the
drivers music
a language i do not know
perhaps arabic
perhaps not
yet if i cannot tell
                    i realize

then neither can
                    those
                    who
                    would

                        harm
                        him
                    its not about me

                                what if i am not
                                the main character?

a post said it better
yesterday—

                        —talking about the spiritual
                        community needing to
                        catch up

                                    they did not expect
                                        the "great
                                        awakening"
                                        to centre
                                    on Palestine

28.

wake up
body tired
no words   scroll the news
     from last night

they kept trudeau
in a restaurant
for hours
until police
escorted
him out   *does this make you*
     uncomfortable?

imagine
the folks
clutching pearls

imagine
what this man felt

     then multiply it
     bodies in the streets
     babies
     the children
     eleven
     thousand
     human beings
     relatives
     spirits
     martyred

i wasnt able to write
this poem
until i got angry
saw a status posted
from someone
denying my family
their rights   their
     work
i am so
tired
of infighting

     i just want to do
     good work
     i just want to do
     good work
     i just want to do
     good work

     what
     when your
     good work
     doesnt matter
     what when
     nothing
     stops
     this genocide
     what when
     all the infighting
     keeps you
     away?

is this truly the legacy
you want to leave your grandchild?
a legacy of anger?
     or one of healing?

a legacy of genocide?
     or one where you
     stood up?

29.

wake up
middle of the night

low blood sugar
excitement
seven years
sober   recognize
          you didnt eat
          enough last night
realize
just like in this
pandemic

          immunocompromised
                in Palestine
             likely means
                  already
                     gone
in the dark   think of your mentor
after a hot shower   panic attacks
after you order   and travel
an uber bike   delays
to bring you food

                              pray for all
          you begin   the Palestinians
     writing next weeks   the children
       disability talk   the amputees
       in your head
                               do you know
                              that during
                               and after
                          (it never really ended
                                did it?)
                            the Iraq "war"
                          (i cannot use these
                              terms lightly
                               anymore)
                           that the science of
                               prosthetics
                               improved?

imagine a world
where every dollar
spent killing people

        helped someone   walk
                                         instead

        helped someone   breathe
                                         instead

        helped someone   stay calm
                                         instead

        helped hold our   frayed
                                         nervous
                                         systems

        helped us
                                         take care
                                               of
                                         each
                                         other

30.

this week
drained me
rewriting
eighty four pages
in twelve hours
travel   nothing i am going
being around   through
people   now
doing something   can compare to those
new   in Palestine

filled me up in   and so
more meaningful ways   i pray   may my own
too   small
will stay   sacrifices
with me   these weeks
for many years   take a bite
                                             out of what
                       as i work   they are feeling
                          to rest
                  my tired body   may my throat
                     i feel the   being dry
                   unfathomable   from the
                        weight   hotel room
                 of these truths   help take

                                            some of that
           i do not know   dryness
               tired   for
           i do not know   any of them
               thirsty
           i do not know
               hunger   for Bisan
           i do not know   for Plestia
               discomfort   for
                                Motaz
                                for
                                Osama
                                for
                                Palestine
                                free

                                            free
                                          Palestine

66

31.

my heart oh my heart
lifts when i read
of dancing in the streets
of Gaza
at word of a
                    truce

my heart
oh my heart
drops at the sight of   as i think of
of another video   what i will say
another photo   tomorrow

                                         as i take a moments
                         dead   rest
                     children   now
                         dead
                       bodies   as i feel my
                         dead   belly
                       babies   full of fry bread
                           so   and tea
                         many   from a
                     unburied   student gathering
                         dead   where many of us
                                         were trans
my heart oh   where we
my heart   crafted
has grown   and coloured
in its capacity   together

                for grief

                                         my heart oh my
                                                heart

                                         has grown in its
                                                capacity

                                                for love

there seems to always
be new
information to
take in

how happy will i be
to hear the words
ceasefire
to know
the bombs will
stop
if only
for a moment
a day
a week

i will not deny us that
joy
that win
we must let it sustain us
we must invite it in
so as to help us
continue

think of all the criticisms
of The Apology™
yet i will never forget
what it meant
for my grandma
what it meant for
the survivors
of those schools

my heart oh my heart
vows to hold
the
complexity

32.

today
we spoke of
disability justice
and
Indigenous
solidarity

    i called upon
    my audience
      for
    a moment of
      silence

    to witness
    and honour
    the people of
    Palestine
    Sudan   until we have a world
    Congo   free of war
    all who are
    experiencing   until we
    genocide   end the occupation
                 end all
we cannot   the occupations
speak of disability
justice
    i told them   until we
              abolish
         the police state

    until we shut down
      the colonial
      capitalist
       war
      machine

    until we can
     imagine
    a world
        where
      all of us
       are
       free

33.

"I cant believe you!
Im going to call the police!
Right now!"

> i am crossing
> the street
> in vancouver
> and a woman
> with a head covering
> is coming the other way

how naive i am
as i see her notice my
keffiyeh
to smile
(perhaps its good
i am masked
and wearing sunglasses)

> she doesnt call the police
> what would she have
> even said?

and afterwards google search
to learn that some
Jewish women
cover their hair
after marriage

> interesting
> to think
> how similar
> these seemingly
> warring cultures
> (too simplified
> i know
> there are many
> many
> praying for peace
> there are
> more than
> two sides
> two religions
> two
> cultures)

> later
> i am speaking
> at an event and see a student
> in the crowd
> notice the keffiyeh
> say something to his friend
> again i find myself
> confused
> he has curly hair
> what do i know
> by looking?

i feel the fear
rise up in me
will he speak?
will he call me out
like she did?
what is he saying?

stop

i hear my thoughts

*if he does
youll say you condemn
all violence
youll say*

*they are my relatives
in Palestine*

*youll
stand up*

he approaches you
to introduce himself
"a big fan" he says
explains hes Kurdish

shares back home
they changed his name
outlawed
his
name

tells me the keffiyeh is
traditional clothing in his
homelands
too

*thank you
for wearing it*

34.

two weeks
on the road
exhausted
try to find time for
rest between
all the things
every day
a list   today   this weekend
              home   a ceasefire
                            not enough
      my warm bed   of course
      my husband   not even close
      our plants
      our dog   nothing can
      our blankets   make up for
      and towels   twenty
      our well   thousand
    giving us water   dead
    at any moment

              and yet

            a video of
           a young boy
          maybe eleven
              smiling
          into the sky
        can you hear that?

no drones
no bombs
no sounds
of war
for four days   let four
                  become
                      for
                      ever

                let them
                go home

35.

last night
i came home
from
another
exhausting
meeting
                    how many times
                     can we ask
                      the elders
                    what we want
                     next year?
                    what we should
                            do?
i am
slowing down

we are
still
losing
people
                        overcome
                    with moments
                    of hopelessness
                    and there you were
                     in my dms   and every time
                                        we message
                                        i think about how
                                        youve said before
                                        that i was there

                                                there i was
                                        we were both so young
                                             i didnt know
                                              your brother
                                               but i knew
                                                  you

i knew that
if our boss at the time
had shown up
it would have been
bumbling

difficult
even then
i knew
somehow
i could hold
whatever grief
i came upon
knocking at your door

now here we are
decades later
and you remind me

it is enough to be existing
sometimes right now

and

STARS EXIST! SAME
TIME AS US

and i decide to honour
all the queers and girls
and boys in Palestine by
doing a full face of makeup

by wearing lipstick for the
first time in years
by wearing a keffiyeh
and an aunty scarf
and my leather collar
to read poems
to send prayers
to other disabled queers
as we held space for
each other

last night

36.

i see their names
and i think   *more*
                     than
                     journalists

          speaking with
          a Palestinian
     anthropology professor
     a couple weeks ago
               at dinner   a friends partner
                             i hadnt met yet

               i use a word i
          only just learned   *parasocial*
                              relationship
                                        i will admit
                                        i dont really know
                                        what it means—will
                                        search more after
                                        this poem

                              what i really want to say
                              is before now
                              i didnt know

                                   your names

                                             i didnt know
                                             your countries
                              i didnt know
                              your faces

                                   your children

                                   your buildings

                                        your trees
                                        (oh the trees!)

before now
i didnt say

Arab
or
Arabic

or
even
Muslim
i didnt know

and now i see
how much of that
unknowing
was orchestrated
how much they
want me to muddy it
"middle east"   now
even   i know better
"terrorist"   i commit to
learning
to saying
Gaza
a thousand
thousand
times
until your ancestors
smile
at my
pronunciation

more
than
journalists

your images
stories
posts
lives
have changed
me

37.

i am
unwell

the last few days

crashing
from travel

that
time of year

i am preparing
to take some time
off

even if i become
quiet
here

know i do not forget you

Palestine

i am continuing
my prayers

you are
always
in my heart

38.

the fire was out this
morning
                            or
nearly out
really
            the coals still
                    burning
so i filled it up
went back to bed

and again
when i got up
it was nearly
out   hope   i am a poet
             is like this   a teacher
             i suppose   a lover of
                                                                   words

                    sometimes
             a hot bed of coals   like the one
             that catches quick   they killed
                                                              two days ago

             sometimes a cold
                          dark   i dont know
                       firebox   how to witness
                  no shred of   each days horror
                  a flame left   the men stripped
                                                                   down

open the door
a little
let the air in   the childrens
                                                                 drawings
                                                                  of war

             find a way to
             take a breath   keep
                                                      fanning the flames
                                                            keep going
                                                   breath on the spark
                                                                  pray
                                                                  pray
                                                                   for
                                                              Palestine

39.

things have
been full
this week   what
         does it mean
         to not
         write a poem?

to release the
next episode
late   it means
         for the first time
         i was invited
         to my home
         first nation
         to talk
         about grief
         and loss

it means holding space
for our humanness and
letting go of
perfection
         the thing about
         sustainability
         is that
         we only know
         we have sustained
         when we have been
         sustaining
         for quite
         some
         time

i dont write poems
out of guilt
nor shame
nor white supremacist
urgency

i write each poem
         for Palestine
         out of love
         for humanity
         for the martyrs
who were killed by
heavy machinery
         while laying
         outside
         a hospital

if your energy
has been
waning
         dark time
         of the year
know that
we are only days
away from
         the returning
         of the light

         commit to
         a breath
         a rest
         and then
         be like the moon

the moon that looks over
us all from river to sea
from here
         to there

waning now yet waxing
         again soon

         light up the night
         for Gaza

40.

a picture
of me
maybe three
or four
        my older sister
      must have picked up
         chicken pox
           at school
in the picture
we are playing with
play dough
        i hold mine up
          in a circle
         looking through
copying
my sister
         both of us
        comfortable
          at home
          with our
           parents

this morning
reading of
a chicken pox
outbreak
          children
        at a Palestinian
          hospital
children
with no
water   some with
           no
          parents

they are killing
the children
they are killing
their parents

         they are killing
           the poets
          the journalists
           the doctors
         they are bombing
           churches
           hospitals
           homes
even today
when i get sick
i reach
for the comforts
of home
        the kind of soup
        my mom would
           make
        a cool popsicle
        for a sore throat

last night
we prayed
and sang
and cried
and feasted
the fire
for Gaza
        this morning
     i pray for the children
        suffering the
          chicken pox
          outbreak

may they have
comfort
may they see
peace
        may they
         grow
         old

41.

we awake
made it safely
through
the darkest
night
                cancelled plans
                    stayed in
                watched the dark
                        come
                    waiting now
                    as it still
                    has yet
                        to go
it is time for me
to turn my focus
elsewhere
for some time

    it has become clear to me
        what my uncle said

a phd in the hands of an
Indigenous person is the best
                        weapon
                        we have
this time
writing poems
witnessing
                    not over

i will keep checking in
my prayers
my songs
our messages of
solidarity

and yet i decided on the
darkest night of the year
that it is time to recommit

                i see the way
                people are being
                    punished

what does it mean for me to
get a phd?

            maybe not much at all
                but in this world
                where so many are
                facing repercussions

the only responsible thing
is to continue
                    to finish
to join the ranks of
academic doctors

                    screaming free
                            free
                        Palestine

                    until we are
                        free

42.

soon it will be christmas day

theres a pull to sadness
                in me
              its been there
           since i was a teen
         maybe even earlier

my family says
i was always
angry
            the foster mother
                  said it
                     too

this year i feel the pull like
the current of the river
when its too high like the
riptide out west
                    in the ocean
and yet
             theres something
                    else here
something   too
about the way
the lights shine
               down
            from the trees

theres this leader
i know
who had some bad
                     very bad
christmas seasons
past
            since he was a child
these days
he makes christmas joy
his mission

i want to believe
there is something to this
            days of rest
      too much food to eat

i want to believe in the
            magic
          the gifts
        the presents

i want to remember Bisan
     and the little girl
        smiling over
          a mirror

        the kids who
   saved their toys on the
       long walk south
           in Gaza

how can we hold space
        for every pain
       and every joy?

how can we be more like
     the earth the animals
the trees that hold the space
for all those years of tears?

    can we pray for years of
            laughter?

43.

o holy night
the stars are brightly
shining

        it is the night
           where
         a child
      an ancestor

           of
         "your"
           dear
       saviour

call on
them
ask them
for help

      was martyred

               to end the war
                   to end
                 the crush
              of capitalism
to bring us hope

it is the night
where a child
went hungry
                       a star
a star
          may every
             star
  no visions of sugar plums
    no cookies for santa
         that shines
         bring a
         breath of
no water no food no justice
no peace
          peace to
         Bethlehem
            in Gaza

o holy night

may every bite of food we
eat

    we look to those stars
      and pray hard
                bring
        a piece of bread
        a cup of soup
  calling on ancestors
    those who went
       hungry
        a water ration
     to someone across
         the world
  who wept so many
     of their own
        tears
may we find it in ourselves
to sing for every child for
every single being who
came to this earth as if
every one of us can help
    when they were
      here

             this
         weary world
          rejoice

44.

as i am waiting in line
the thought comes
you havent written a
poem
       in a couple of days
you did
however
       play with a baby
      hug your husbands
           cousin
          goodbye
     snuggled the dog
         more
each of these things
bringing
pal eh steen
with you

in the line up the man
behind you is making loud
noises talking to himself a
bit the woman in front of
you pays with nickels
from a change purse

every moment brings
a thought
of gah zah
      our baby niece
       laughing and
         splashing
    with my husband
       in the pool
me holding
her tiny hands
and toes

   my heart full of love for her
  and grief for the babies lost in
         gah zah

the man in the line
behind me
turns out to be
an impatient
older
white man

the person at the till
glances nervously

and i think about all the
neurodivergence in gah
zah

i think about how many
survivors may have
impatience
tics
may
talk to themselves

if they live

please
let
them
live

45.

i raised this tree
like my own child
dont cut it   *shoot me*
            but dont cut it

when we built a fence
i kept telling people
it was life changing

           who knew i would feel
            safer with this fence
              surrounding me

there is an old tree in
the yard
            another one
        just beyond the fence
          that one older
             evergreen

we are growing
into our home
the fence allowing
me
          with my depression
           and panic attacks
to also
grow into   the yard

when we built the fence it
created this space for me
for my
         neurodivergent brain

the smell of the cedar i talked
to the trees and the bushes as
i stained that fence i talked
to them of how i knew it was
their relative and why i was
using this stain to protect it

my husband talked to
and moved each spider
out of the way of the stain

we didnt grow either tree
likely i wasnt even alive
when either was a seedling

we werent here when the
blue jays hatched

unlike the man in the video
        the man there in gah zah
                in pal ah steen

        and yet i understand the
        grief in ways i now under-
stand how the fence brought
                me comfort

the space between those
who would cut the tree
would shoot the man
who wouldnt
miss
the
birds

                        and those of us
                who would die for the tree
                        those of us who
                relate better to the trees in
                our yards than perhaps
                        anyone

46.

wake up
in pain   the first poem
                  i wrote
                 for Palestine
               i was in pain
                     too
at what point
does pain become
chronic?

should i
go back on
meds?   *was it*
           something
             i ate?   *am i*
                   making it
                    all up?
all these thoughts
fears
as we dont make it
to the ceremony
          because i need to
              attend to
            the very real
                  pain
                 illness
                 upset
              stomach

i can feel the pull of
thoughts i didnt think i
would have anymore
remember any sniffle a
couple years ago being
immediate cancelled plans
and i can see how the shift
in the way people think
happens slowly over time
we decide something just
doesnt matter anymore

as i ponder all this
the feeling that
                i should be there
makes me think of the
title of my book
             you are enough

every time
i cannot *do*
i am overcome
still feel
a failure   and
yet
        i am learning from
      revolutionary movements
         that sometimes
           not doing
    not working not buying
      not participating
        is enough or
          it will be
enough
if you keep adding
if you keep
sustainability at the heart
of how we move forward
together   pause
          rest
pick it up   again
            keep
            going

47.

still sick
today

my stomach churning
had therapy though

                and commented
                       on a post
                   about a play
        they are still choosing to
                             run
                      in spite of
                   it being written
                 by a white man
              with no connection
                      to the lands
                       where the
        "conflict" is happening

this world that hates conflict
this world that has trained us
to always move away from
pain or towards pleasure which
i learned in the context of sell
sell—
           —sell   everything
                         an item
                  to be owned

                      the land
                      the land
                 the olive trees

today i read about a healer in
Hlathikhulul who was gifted land
by community to connect with
harvest and help others on

            but what about paperwork?
            his wife couldnt stop herself
                      from asking

                  what if something
                        happens?

something is always happening

someone is always being removed
from their lands

mortgages go unpaid and houses
       get foreclosed and nobody
understands that the paperwork
                   protects no
                           body
so many
bodies
unprotected by
paperwork—
             —paperwork that could
                    stop the bombs
                is the only paperwork
                             i care
                            about
                              now
something is always
happening

                      a genocide
                     a kidnapping
                       a bombing
                        a murder

48.

i wake before five am
most days
            in the dark
        while my husband sleeps
        the glow of this phone
            shows me
                the news
                of the day
dont get distracted
a text from yesterday
echoes   as my
            depression lingers
                as my
        anger is burning coals
        in the pit of my stomach
        reminding me of my
                    humanity

        is believing in something
    more human than losing all
                hope?

this   morning   i   read   about
far   too   many   white   men
and   it   strikes   me   that
no matter how much i believe
we   are   all   waking   up
there are still too many stories
by   and   for   and   about
white men

one of my buddhist
acquaintances (friends?)
                therapist
said to me once in what felt like
an oddly flippant tone

                its going to get worse
                for two thousand years
                before it gets better

i remember being confused
by the confidence

                whats it like to feel so
                    certain?

                its a few days into my
        commitment to my phd and
        the apathy is getting to me
                    again

this is where i usually set
things aside

i can feel the familiar pull of
all the horrible things in the
world can feel the dragging
of the undertow

            whats the fucking point?

today i read about civilian
deaths in the
Iraq war
                today i read about
                    Vietnam
            today i read about
                    Palestine
        and i know i need to fan the
                embers of hope
                    again
know i need to
find something to help me
keep going

49.

today marks
six months
since the day
we got married

our friends
and family
making their way
over the mountains
across the water
down the winding road
to the
edge of the island

marrying my
best friend
at my
dream wedding
on the beach
where the ocean
begins
and doesnt end
until its
across
the world

        across
        the world

today
marks
three months
since the day
they use
as their
justification
for
the continuing
genocide
of
Palestinians
in Gaza

      how do i hold this dichotomy
                 within me?

      the same way i kept going
      after our mother left
      twenty twenty four
      will mark

                  six years
                  since then

        i read today of a couple
          who was married
           october fifth
            whose love
              resists
              defies
            liberates
         may Palestine
        come to know
      more happy anniversaries
      than they can count
        more than these
          devastating
           numbers
              of
             loss

may the
thirty thousand
spirits
be free
may the living
be freed
               before
             another
             three
             days
          six months
     seventy five years
             goes
             by

50.

no poems
feel like coming
as we wait
and watch
      South Africa
      is leading us
      into this
      new place
we will find
ourselves
again
at a
turning point
                              today i saw
                          one of those
                    meaningless
      when i teach   (likely used for
      about   ai training)
      reconciliation   posts
      i say
      post a photo
its a   *of when you*
line   *were twenty four*
within   *in honour*
each of   *of 2024*
us
      there is a
      line   became compelled
      to scroll through
      more than a decade
there comes   of photos
a moment   to find
where we must   her
      take sides   kissing the
where the test   camera
of what we face   drunk
becomes too large   in saskatoon
      when
      what we stand for   and i realize then that i am
      must become   hoping in spite of it all
      more   that the next more than a
      than   decade changes the world
      metaphor   as much as this last one
      changed me

51.

wake up
cold
the "snap"   has started
                prayers
           for relatives
              with no
      overnight warming
                rooms
realize i dont
know much
about the
seasons
in Palestine

             is it like our   today i cried
               bc desert?   feeling abandoned
     Secwepmc territory?   a tiny moment
     where fires burn hot   triggering my
               in summer   loneliness
       and a dry cold   trauma
        frost comes in
        these days?   recognizing
visit the cats   how much we are
in their room   holding
where i always turn
the space heater on
and my husband   *why am i anxious?*
always turns   theres no need to make up
it off   think of   a reason
             stray
             cats   there are so many
think of   good reasons
     the image   to feel this panic
    from yesterday   as gentle
  or the day before—   loving
                souls
               are martyred
  —a young Palestinian
         man   as people who deserve
     bottle feeding   to live
       a kitten   try to find
such gentle loving care   some warmth

52.

it doesnt matter
what we try

every poem
i feel the
pull to
hope

        and then
           every
        tiny hope
      feels dashed
the
arguments
the fighting
the bombing
the debates
the conflict
the conflict
the conflict
           in all of it
     what surprises me the
              most
                is
       what people
             can
         survive
i remember
a long time
ago
a medicine person
we asked
about suicide

    when there are all kinds of
        people who
        want to live

      the statement stayed
           with me

today i wonder
if i got
cancer
or some other
illness that
was leading to
death
          if i was in
          Palestine
            even

    would i become
   someone who wants
      to live?

dont go worrying
its been a lifetime
of this
         no need
        for crisis
          mode
just a lingering
wondering
what it would be
like
       to be someone
     who didnt have to
          fight
        so hard
       to want
         to
        stay

   a lingering question of
  whether i should even
  post this poem if theres
 no fight in it if theres no
hope in it then whats the
          point?

53.

the hospital
the hospital

somewhere i saw
its the
last
hospital
                somewhere i saw
                        a man
                telling us the story
                        of his
                        daughter
                he is a surgeon
                she has been
                        wounded

            the hospital
            the hospital

no anaesthesia
amputated
without
anaesthesia
                    just last week
                i was on a zoom
                talking about
                prescribed
                    safer
                    supply

we are beginning to see
how when humans feel
this incredible amount of
pain that they will seek
help one of the doctors
we spoke with talked of
his own recognition that
he could not fathom their
pain
            their pain

we work to help people
survive
                    their pain

what if we could change the
world so that pain wasnt so
        deep?

earlier today
i read about   *soul*
                       loss
my osteopath
and i talked about
it last week
too—
            —do souls come here
                    truly evil?
not in my teachings
                        i said
but we can continue to make
choices
            as i understand it
that put holes in our spirits
                        or
that send our spirits away as
something else
takes over

brush your shoulders off
clean up and pray weep
and hold space for the
pain call yourself back call
yourself back and witness
choose the actions that
contribute to life today
always honour and make
offerings to life and love
and remember your spirit
so it stays with you always

54.

i take a bath
i pray for Gaza
i stack the wood
i pray for Gaza
i eat breakfast
i pray for Gaza
i snuggle with my pets
i pray for Gaza
i visit my family
i pray for Gaza
i drive my car
i pray for Gaza
i burn my hand
i pray for Gaza
i wake up
i pray for Gaza
i open my computer
i pray for Gaza
i brush my teeth
i pray for Gaza
i say "i love you"

i pray
i pray
i pray
for Gaza

55.

dear Motaz

what words are there
to tell you
we are grateful
for you   we cant
imagine
            how hard it was
            to make the choice

   i saw some say they are
   grateful you are alive
            and i am
               too

               i am
            grateful
            for your
               life
and yet
i imagine hearing that
bringing the pain
of every death
you
witnessed
                        you
                        alive

               and so many
                  of your
                  people
                     not

as the morning comes
here in the dark
across the world
i wonder

               where will you
                        go?

a couple summers ago
i remember being so
angry
   *there is nowhere i can go that
         whiteness hasnt touched*
even deep in
forests where
Indigenous peoples
try not to be found

                     missionaries
                     take their
                        boats
                           their
                     big trucks
i hope
dearest Motaz
wherever you take in the
next sunrise
that there is
quiet
            and then i think
               how unsettling
               the quiet may feel
               *may it bring
                     relief
                  may your
                     body
                     find
                     rest*
dear Motaz
i have no words really
to honour this journey
perhaps

            *we will remember you
            we will say your name*

                     enough

56.

i can feel it in me
the pull to urgency

posts about
the courts

        wanting
        to know

why didnt they
say ceasefire?

        the pull
        to emotion
should i feel
deep disappointment?
celebration?
the only two things
my brain
wants

        look for a post
        that challenges
           this
           binary
look for some truth
for someone
who understands this
more
than
me

      the court
      stopped short
      of ordering
      a ceasefire

        but the findings
        are nevertheless
        damning

        for israel

let us take a collective
breath
        this morning

      let us take
      the sacred pause

as the day
goes on
theres sure to be
more
        hot takes
more
        anger
        fear
      perhaps even
     some semblance
        of
        joy
let us not get
too caught up
the work continues

     until dawn comes
       over a
        free
       Palestine

57.

the stars
look down
and dont
recognize
Gaza
anymore
        or do they
        or do they

there was a time
when
everything
everything
everything

    happened
    for a
            reason

a time when even though
our mother died i could
find ways to say it was
okay it was okay it was

            never
            okay
            i
            am
not
okay

            when
            that
            rich
            rich
            man
            was (is)
    blowing rockets up
        in the sky
    making new stars
        in the sky

        when i saw it
        for the first
            time
        i shouted
    pull over the car
            what is it
            what is it

    the heavens
    changed
    a straight line
    of satellites
    across
    the sky
    the sky

    the sky is
    changing
    the stars
    are changing

    the sky
    in bombs
and evacuation
    letters
    falls on
    Gaza

    the sky
    the sky
    the bombs
have changed
    the earth
    so greatly
    in Gaza
    in Gaza
we can see it
    from
            the sky

58.

i am not well
today

try to find words
trigger
self sabotage
trauma
                    and yet
                    and yet

        there is a genocide
            happening
            in Gaza   keep love at the centre

how is   love
                    anyone   that is so
            well?   deeply
                                                woven into
                                                        this
i want to turn off all my   pain
feelings
                    want to   i ask you to learn
                    numb it out   how to hold discomfort
want to   for we are
push it   tired
away   we are
                                     tired
            worrying myself   of holding all this
                as i feel   pain
                jealous   ourselves
                envious
                of those   this pain they continue to
                going on   cause so they can have
                with their   their money their wealth
                days   their resources i cannot
                                 understand it i cannot i
                                 am not i cannot i am not

                                            well
                                            today

59.

they are flooding the tunnels
with seawater
making the ocean

       the ocean
       the water
         our
       mother

         into a weapon

                years and years ago
                 my best friend
             who i barely knew then
             got in a car with me
                we drove
             thousands of miles
             to standing rock
                to pray

         i wrote a poem
           there

                talking of how they used
                dogs
                our medicine
                against us

                how weapons come from the
                land

       the land
         amak
      our bodies
       the land
      our bodies
       the land
      our bodies

years ago i walked in
vancouver
with thousands
tens of thousands
maybe even
a hundred
thousand   we walked
                    after hearing
        chief robert joseph say

namwayut
we are all one
                        we are all
                            one
we are all
                    from water

water is the first thing
that comes
before a baby is to
                        be born
come   they are using
        earthside   our sacred waters
                                                to destroy
                                                    Gaza
                from the stars

                                        today we will pray
a list of   five hundred of us
baby names   online
age of death: on a computer screen
                zero years old
                zero years old   may our prayers reach the
                zero years old   ocean may our prayers take a
                                        bite out of it may our prayers
                                         continue to build a world
                                        where the ocean is the ocean
                                        and never again

                                                a weapon

60.

yesterday
i read a post
from a local fruit farm

            one
       hundred
       percent
       bud loss

there was a
cold snap
and all the   soft
                fruit
                trees   lost
                         this years
                         harvest

       i am no arborist
          no farmer
          no gardener

our house plants are alive
solely due to my husband
and his commitment to
watering them every week
without fail though i do sing
to them
                   sometimes

      i saw a map of Gaza
         with every
           building
        that had been
      turned to rubble
       marked by a
       tiny red dot   what of the trees?

yesterday
i got curious (some
combination of
neurodivergence and my
venus in gemini)

went down a
google trail
about the
history of lube   i learned
                     centuries ago
                     they used
                     olive oil

meditating a moment
on fruit and oil and love and
sensuality

the feel of biting into a plum
a strawberry a peach
juice dripping down your
chin the sweetness oh

sweet

what sweetness
do the children of Gaza
remember?
what sweetness left
between lovers?

as the buds froze
in ʔamakʔis Ktunaxa

across the earth
the colonizers
burn the olive trees

the people
live in tents
make
coats from
military blankets

and i pray for the trees for
the lovers for the children
for the sweetness to

return home
home
to Gaza

61.

the other day
we found a seat
in the airport
near a gender neutral
washroom
(thanks
at least
for that
alberta ndp)
        at some point
        i noticed
        a Muslim man
        had chosen
        a corner nearby
        to honour
        his prayers

i know so little of Islam
been learning the odd bit
here and
there
since i started paying
more
attention   since i
        realized
        what was happening
        in Gaza

        since i began
        to understand
        the sacrifices
        made
        for faith

as he bowed and prayed
and rose again
i thought of our own
dances
songs
prayers

we face our lodges
        east
        i wondered
        if they pray
        facing east
        too
but mostly
        i watched the people
        around him
i decided
if anyone tried to
disturb this mans prayer
i would get up

        i would have opened my
        drum bag
        i would have sang
        and prayed
        and done anything i could
        to protect him

he finished his prayers
with no incidents
i ate my lunch
we boarded the plane
as we landed i heard the
old lady across the aisle
from him ask about his
book—
        —she was Mennonite
        i think
its in Arabic
he said

        and as we waited for
        our luggage
        i saw him rush to help
        her and her companions
        lift their bags up off the
        line

62.

wake up
feel the tired
in my body   lately
        its the kind
        from doing
        the good work
spent two days
in my old role
shkaabewis
helper   waking up
        in the dark
        greeting
        the sun
        with
        hundreds of
        others

sunrise ceremony always lifts
my heart yet right after
saturdays prayers i opened my
phone to the news of Hind oh
dearest Hind oh dearest Reem
souls of our souls my heart oh
my everbreaking   heart

i returned to this gathering of
elders of knowledge holders
to talk about love
and loss   to honour and
        hold space for
        grief
on the first day
i opened space for
people to share their
grief stories
        discomfort
filled the room people left
people refilled their coffees
people   chatted
about   the weather

how do we get you to
expand your ability to hold
discomfort and pain? it is
the only way i know and
yet   and yet

        you dont even turn
        off
        your
        tv
racism wont stop you
genocide
wont
stop you
your dissociation
is killing our
planet
your dissociation
is killing
brown
babies   my heart
        oh
        my ever
        breaking
        heart

may this grief i feel never
numb may we pray harder
and learn to let go of small
comforts in the face of
injustice may we all break
free may we all may we all free
free Palestine

63.

wake up
body
sore
again

        travel seems to
          take more
          and more
         out of me

especially
as i reflect
on the planes
that drop
bombs
on the
companies
their glowing
logos surrounding me

        and how they
         contribute
            to
          genocide

last night we picked up the
car and drove through the
snow to get home
home

        home

            woke up
            warm
          in our bed

this morning i felt delight
as i walked over to the
window and saw how the
light is returning the light
is returning the way the
sky looks at sunrise feels
like it used to for just a
moment and i know we
are surviving the winter
this winter that didnt get
cold enough

        my heart turns to
      concern for a second
          the beings
         on the land
        that needed
         the cold
       the drought
       the drought
  the promise of a season
of fires rivalling the one
before that and the one
          before
           that

and my heart
finds its way back to
                    Gaza   to Rafah

how do the Palestinian
people feel at another
        sunrise?

how do they handle the
smoke from the bombs?
the way we take cover in
        summer?
    from the smoke
    from the fires

    there are only tents
    there is no water
    they bombed the safe
    zones they murdered the
        children

                        and some racist on the
                        west coast writes an op ed
                        and our prime minister
                        tweets about anti semitism
                        and i am grateful for the
                        sun rise and yet in it i see a
                        young Palestinian girl her
                        life her death and i beg the
                        sun the stars the trees the
                        water i beg my ancestors
                        stop it now please end it
                        now   ceasefire   ceasefire
                        end the genocide save the
                        children do something we
                        must do
                                    something

64.

rest
rest
rest
       trust in
       another
       comrade
to keep holding it down

       just for a moment
while
you
rest   an anti
       colonial
       therapist
       you follow

writes that its not time for
the conversation now
(people in Gaza are
still being martyred the
situation in Gaza still
as urgent as the day you
wrote your first poem)

two years ago
(actually four
pandemic time
is crip time
is time   real?)

       i was diagnosed
       with adhd
       went on
       and off
       meds
nothing giving me
       stability
       stability
what helps me
       stabilize?

the other night the smoke
alarm went off and my
nervous system my
nervous system is frayed
already and i was so angry

imagine each persons
nervous system in Gaza

i saw a video of a young
girl in the rain she was
terrified
the thunderers were
visiting
but of course
she has flashbacks
to the
bombing
the never
ending
bombing

that therapist mentioned
what it feels like for
colonized bodies
to be witnessing a colonial
genocide
in real time
our bodies remember
their bodies
will remember

i pray for a ceasefire
for peace
for the chance
of a traumatized body
to know
rest
rest
rest

65.

a poem for Nex
and for every
nonbinary
Palestinian
youth
whose names we
did not get to
learn

            when i get
              starworld

                                    uncle smokii
i will post up   will find a good
somewhere   big
                                        flat
see some image from when i   warm
had to go to catechism (back   rock
before my mom went to
university and learned about   up there in the stars
our own stories—grandma
a residential school survivor and well sit together well
—you know us complicated   sit in circles well visit and
catholics) some image of jesus drink tea
posted up on a rock   *why not now*
surrounded by kids and ·
lambs or maybe it was saint my heart whispers
francis   there are so many things
                                       to be done on this
                                       earthly plane

                                       because
                                       Nex was
                                       murdered

                                       because
                                   young girls
                                     did this
                     because
                     the young ones
                     in Gaza
                     were martyred before they
                     could even ask who they
                                   might
                                    become

```
        let me become someone
                  who wanders
        the mirror of starworld
                   here on earth
        asking each one of you
                     queer kids
                    your name
your name
the one you chose
the one you offer
the one that brings a
unicorn
sparkle
to your
eyes                          your
                             heart


the other day in the grocery
store a small yet mighty voice
called out *i LOVE your HAIR*
and their mom asked if they
saw the teal underneath and i
showed them the teal in the
front and they showed me
*see? i have the side of my head
shaved too!*
```

oh Nex i see you i see you i
see you our dear Nex may you
rest now may we meet again
in safety in a space where
nothing can touch you but
the light of the star that you
are i see you Nex i see you and
will sit with you and we will
listen to every name for every
martyred being that never
got to tell them to anyone

66.

read a post
about adhd

scroll
a post
where

read a stat
children
as
young
as
five
years
old

i started this poem yesterday
and i have nothing left to say
and i am overcome with the
pain of seeing the eyes stare
back at me from screens the
eyes the eyelids the eyes the
eyelids i can still see Reems
grandfather closing her eyes
their eyes theyre cries for
help i am planning to perform
at a music festival this fall and
how can we be emailing about
this how can i be thinking
about any of this how can i go
on?

told the doctors
they wanted
to die

*ive come to accept
depression as a roommate
as something i will deal with
for a
lifetime*

and yet
there are things
i cannot

today i watched
children do a childrens
activity
surrounded by adoring
parents

i can
not

i
will
not

a mother and a father
recording their child in
tandem as they took their
moment

accept genocide as a
roommate as a global citizen
as a "neighbour" they always
want to say and i correct them

a relation

how can these moments be so
vastly different how can one
human being be searching for
their child among rubble instead
of searching for their child in
the crowd of other children each
doing something a little bit scary
but something they love to do

i do not accept the genocide
of my relations of our
relations in G a z a in
fa lah steen

67.

Mansours own mother
posting to an instagram
story

> *the truth*
> *about stories*
> *is thats all we are*[13]

Aaron Bushnell
set himself on fire
in front of the israeli embassy
in washington dc

> *if you cant*
> *meditate for ten minutes*
> *you need to meditate*
> *for twenty*

Nex Benedict
Tina Fontaine
Colten Boushie
Hodan Hashi
Ahmaud Arbery
Trayvon Martin   Reem
                      Hind
                      Saleem
                      Refaat
and we keep asking
ourselves

> *what helps with this?*
> *why do i feel like this?*

book in with a nutritionist
move the tv into the other
room sit down to write
sit down to write but
check an email and go to
your generative somatic
zoom group and decide
youll go talk to the
"homecomers" this weekend
while your husband goes
to visit his friend in the
hospital in the hospital

when my dad met that friend
at the wedding he had so
much to say about imagining
what life must be like as a
trans person you know the
way too many people think
pity is empathy

> and there it is a line
> you wonder if youll
> delete

only really censor
yourself
when it comes to
family

but what about that
thomas king quote
surely someone will say
dont quote that
fake

> just like well discuss the
> nuance of anti Blackness
> when an occupied Palestinian
> makes a comment

and yet in dc Aaron set himself
on fire and here in our yard
the wind scares the dog so he
gets to sleep with us in the
night whose bed do we go to
when were this scared of the
world? should we all be like
Aaron? should we go back on
medication? what should we
do with all

> these
> names?

68.

another child
in thunder bay
has died
                    belgium is
          revoking citizenship of
                Palestinian children

canada is
supporting the
new war

              what will they call it?
                "the red sea war?"

where Yemen is
protecting
Palestine   and we
                      the people
                      have no say
                as our governments
                        sign up
                    to continue
                    the genocide
                    the removal
                            the
                        killing
another child
has died
                and somehow
                i still ordered
                    an ipad
even as i know   today
                there is blood
                on my hands

          we want a good life for
                ourselves

            we deserve to be
                elders

and today the only route
to elderhood i can
imagine is one where i
continue to learn how to
draw and then where i
sell those drawings on
some sort of product to
some willing customer
because i truly dont
know if anything else can
be sustainable
                        i want to
                        imagine
                        otherwise
i need to
believe theres a
way out
                    i need to trust
                    theres things
                    we can
                    do
and yet
and yet

          lately i think of my
            grandma
          her little life
          the way she liked
            to gamble
          and eat sweets

                    what is enough
                        for me?
                    what will be the joy
                    people remember
                    i gave them?
                    is it enough?
can it ever
              be
                    enough?

69.

are you ok?
whats wrong?
whats happening?

the only word
i can feel
as people who
have never
responded
or reshared
a single
post
about
genocide
yet find a way
to worry
about
me
the
individual
is
interesting

there are so many in this
world that have no idea what
is going on and i dont know
how to say

i am not okay i am not okay
i   am   not   okay
without inciting panic in
people who believe that being
okay is more important than
thirty thousand lives
                              nearly
thirty
              thousand
                              deaths

should i be writing back?

what happened is that i learned the
word self immolation in the context
of 2024 and also learned this
wasnt the first person to do this
since i started writing these poems
and i have been living under
colonial occupation my whole life
and it feels pointless to say any of
this because i dont believe youll
understand

i would rather
write back to
the young journalist
asking for an interview
willing to engage me in
the hard questions
of this world
of this life

the compassion in me
(when its accessible)
remembers not knowing
remembers googling
              iz ray el and pah le stine

(sound it out
              i wrote it this way
in the hopes the algorithm
lets you see this post and
not just my sad selfies)

i remember believing it too
complex i remember giving up
on trying to learn
              but its not too late
              no im not okay
are you sure you should
              be?

70.

al shifa hospital is
burning
                    my husband
            is in another city
            visiting a friend
            who has been
            hospitalized
                    for
            two months
we worry
for their care
we worry for
their
rare illness
we pray for their
wellbeing

        and yet we never worry
        they will be bombed
            we never worry
        that the hospital
            will burn

al-shifa hospital
is burning
            on a video i   al shifa hospital is
            couldnt watch   burning
            so i came here   in another city
            to tell you   my friend texts
            i came here to   from an emergency room
            poem   they are concerned about a
                                    recurring health issue

                                    and i worry for them
                                        i pray it goes well
                                        yet i never worry
                                    they will be bombed
                                        i never worry
                                    that the hospital
                                        will burn

al shifa hospital
is burning

the hospital the aid trucks
the houses the tents the
sea the river the field of
olive trees the mosque the
churches the schools
everywhere they go they
are being bombed and
murdered killed martyred
and i cannot understand
this where do you go
when nowhere is safe?

they are calling yesterday

> *the flour massacre*
> *the bread massacre*
> *the flour massacre*

and my naturopath
tells me to eat
good rye bread

> and i want to scream
> not at her
> but at every person
> in the world

how can i get this rye
bread to Palestine why
didnt i become a pilot
how would i even get
over there would they just
shoot me down?

it all feels so
far away

> yet it is
> this close

the light in me is the light
in you us the light going
out in the eyes of a child
in Gaza is the light of the
stars in the sky should be
the lights of a hospital the
light of a safe place the
light of a permanent
ceasefire oh—let Gaza live
we pray we beg we weep

let Gaza live

71.

the elders
and the babies
are dying
of starvation
in Gaza

yesterday
after the elders
meeting
here in our territory

in the lands of
our ancestors

there were
so many leftovers
diligently wrapped up
taken home
shared with people
in the offices

in Gaza
the babies
and the elders
are being
starved   to
death   yesterday
the elders
brought their
photo albums

the photo albums
of Gaza
are under the rubble
the photos are torn apart
by rockets the
houses have been
razed
the churches
the hospitals
the community halls

i think of their
future ancestors

two hundred
three hundred
years from
now
will they look over
every photo left
of their people—
of their cities—
for resemblance
for family?
what historians
will survive
this genocide?
what stories will
they tell?

years ago
at one of my
first
elders
meetings

they taught me
the name they
knew
my grandmother
by

and one elder said "oh
i have a picture of her"

—only the second photo
i had ever
seen

72.

i havent been able to write
since i saw what it looks like
when a person is run over by
a tank

i havent been able
to watch that
full video
i raise my hands
to you
i bow my head
i read about
your
sixteen hour
imprisonment
i think of those
still inside

there is an urgency
to this culture
the culture of
colonialism
and capitalism
that cannot understand
why i may want to
lie down
for a year

day in day out day in day
out abolitionism is a state
of mind free Palestine is a
heartbeat call i can hear
the low hum of your voice
through the photo of you
on stage i know we must
be like mycelium and so
when i read you cant
write

think of how
you didnt post
for international
womens day
think of how
someone told you
your feminist lens
was broken

i write

the first time
i saw the nuances
of indigenous women
really captured
was reading
katherina vermettes
the break

i read it
around the same time
as *birdie* (by tracey
lindberg)

feminism isnt my word so
i guess its okay if my lens
is broken in your eyes

what of a revolutionary
lens?

what of a
lens of
love?

i wonder
how many of the
girls in Gaza
will grow up to be writers
will honour the nuance
of the relationships
between their
mothers
and grandmothers

will
write an ode
to grieving
to fasting

to women
who lie down
for a
year
in ceremony

will they find ways to
grieve these losses
and write their
stories?

or was Hind to
become that
writer? was
Reem?

73.

when i listen to Bisans
videos
even for fifteen seconds

the buzzing sound
of the planes
the drones
the war machines
is what stands out
most

my neurodivergent
brain
cannot listen for
long
without wanting to
smash my phone

i have witnessed
sun dancers
have seen
young women
put out
for their
four days

what if i did?
or
what if i was in Gaza?

when i think about that
sound the constant
buzzing the droning the
sounds of war on and on
and on

how can i even
imagine
what it must be like

i think of how we would
sing and drum on the
other side of the trees for
the fasters to hear
i think of how we would
sing and drum to help the
dancers

day in
day out
day in

i am not Muslim
i have no experience with
Ramadan

ceasefire for gods sake for
the fasters sake let them
pray in the peace of a
silent mosque let them
pray without the sky
opening up and raining
death upon them

i do know
what its like
to support
those
fasting

74.

the seasons
are changing
the urgency
of a newly
awoken
nervous system
slowing
         in october
      we saw things
       we deemed
       unimaginable

in november
we spent time
learning
         nakba
         1948
       olive trees
     settler colonialism
       the flag
     the watermelon
   an image from a time
     when the flag
      was banned

yesterday i listened
to a podcast on
fraudsters
yesterday
i listened to the
Black folks
posting

         when our warrior mom
           was still here
             earthside
               alive
          she would tell us
           be wary of fame

     she talked about fame
     the same way she talked
     of alcohol
     of that other thing
     the voracious ones
     she called them

            the spirits
            that only
             know
             how to
              take

yesterday i unfollowed a
few accounts

and i realize that i am
feeling the fear of what its
like to have done nothing

i realize that even a book
of poems doesnt appease
this hunger inside of me
for justice for freedom for
an end to occupation

my mentor tells me
i notice occupation
like a magnet
wrote a whole series
on consent

watched a video today
of a covid conscious
person talking about their
refusal to consent to the
occupation of their body
from the germs of others
and i see it
and yet
i dont know if i will wear
a mask tomorrow
and yet
i continue to fall
short
and yet
and yet
and yet

75.

and then i remember
i see a video
of millions
in the streets

       where is this?
    one commenter asks

    worldwide

world
             wide

    world
    wide
            world
wide

and i see a video
of an elder woman
a grandmother
an aunty
in South Africa

our love of each other as
wide as this whole world
as long and as great as the
circumference of the earth
the distance a mother truly
means when she says *i love
you*

        to the moon
        and back

(i wonder just now what
the name of that place is
in the mouths of the
people who survived who
are still there who are that
land whose bodies and
childrens bodies came
from the earth there
whose ancestors returned
to the earth there)

she tells us
this is
about life
about justice
about
fighting
colonialism

        world
        wide

remember remember

                i am a poet
                every word
            an association

                      they call the way my brain
                      makes connections a
                      deficit they call it a
                      disorder so that they can
                      have me questioning
                      myself my heart my
                      associations with words
                      so that they can control
                      me

                              remember when
                              we called it

                      The World Wide Web™?

does gen z know it was supposed
to be free? does alpha? do you
know the first creators of internet
wanted it open source remember
when wikipedia didnt need to
beg for our funds remember when
ads werent a thing? only on tv?
remember remember remember

                              remember
                              the world
                              can
                              change

76.

yesterday i wrote my
seventy fifth poem

today number seventy six

2024
marks seventy six
years

since the
nakba

        this morning
        i signed a petition
        for bc schools
        to teach the
        nakba

reconciliation
is
dead

and then i saw an image of a
star of david carved into the
back of a Palestinian by an
iz rae lee soldier and i dont
know how to reconcile that
with the information i was
taught in bc schools about
genocide about that star

a banner i saw
in Wet'suwet'en
a banner the police had
to rip through to arrest
our grandmother as they
prayed for Yintah
as they prayed for their
territories blood and their
veins and their bodies

we are the land

its not a metaphor we are
the blood of the being that
fell whose body became
the mountains we are the
land our blood is the water

we are all connected

they blow holes in the
landscape as they do to
Palestinian bodies they
are destroying whole
ecosystems whole villages
whole beings whole
families whole bloodlines
whole babies

seventy six years
of resistance

five hundred
and thirty two
years
of resistance

we are the land we return
to the land we become
the stars and come back
again and you cannot
remove us your greed
cannot continue we will
not stop *from the river to the*
see until Palestine and the rest
of the world

are free

77.

four days since
you posted your last
poem
        you said
        you couldnt
        hold space
        in prayer
        this weekend
        either

made it your mission to
honour the life you are in
with presence this
weekend knowing your
husband will leave soon to
go north with his nephew
to visit friends and to see
another place his dad
loved when he was still
here
      present on this earth

      i have to trust
        the lulls
    the space between
          words
       on the page

i have to trust the
absence
        sometimes
    as much as the
       presence

yesterday
all the cards you
pulled
in the somatic
therapy
session
talked
of
trust

   i dont have any answers

the cards
talked
about   the
                divine
             feminine
               and
            masculine
the star
of venus

sacred androgyne

      its
     always
     both
          and

hold the complexities

i have to trust that
the peace i felt
standing in the sunlight
of my backyard
made its way
to the heart
of a child
in Gaza

because i asked it to
because i sent that prayer
because sometimes
i feel crazy

because
i have been asking
if i am
if i was
that time
i saw what
might become
the future

i have to trust my
presence here in this life
this love this body this
home this yard
matters just as much as
my practice of
presence

i have to trust we can
take a bite out of it
just like the warmth of
spring has found its way
back to us just like the
old stories say we can

with what is happening
there in that place that
knows too much death
too much hunger too
much loss

seek balance
pray for
peace

78.

today is your birthday
every year
it strikes me how
unexpected grief comes

          some birthdays
       i prepare for a landslide
         and its just small
              lapping
                waves

today
as i commit to finishing
what i started
as i try to
just write the damn thing

         i am crushed
        under the weight
       of reading theory
    that we would have talked
        about for hours

i want to sit on our porch
and smoke with you
sit after sweat
share stories
and silence

     i am a completely changed
         person

          this is what
       dehumanization
            does
this is what
genocide
does

so many funerals that as
they bury one the next
casket is brought into the
gym for the wake—

     —so many bodies and
      they are still being
martyred violently shot at
and killed while they try
to retrieve the bodies that
          have fallen
i think about
what a privilege
it was
to take that
time   grief takes
           so much
             time
after she left us
i started to have panic
attacks every time a family
member left i used to believe
one of us was going to die at
any moment
          how are they
       to sleep in Gaza
   when that is their truth?

i still worry
i still miss you
im still not done the damn
thing yet

        i am working on it
        i am working on it
           i am working

but what of those with no
time to grieve?

79.

one million people
one
point
one million   people
                 children
                 babies
                 mothers
                 sisters
                 cousins
                 uncles
                 brothers

       at risk of starvation

today
a cbc interviewer
has asked me
to write this poem
on air
            they are
      asking me about
            poems
              as
            protest

how i wish
i could say   *each word*
            i wrote
     stopped a bomb
       from falling
         stopped a
           child
         from dying

how i pray
each word
      turned into a
      bird singing
    in a clear blue sky
         in Gaza

how i imagine
each word
turning into
nourishment
food and water
a warm hug
from a
living
mother
           yet what can i
           really tell you?!

i write these poems
selfishly
to feel better
to hold out hope

           they shared
           of a man
           who lit a candle
           every day
           outside the
           presidents house
           during Vietnam
           when asked he says

     i know it might not change
     them but im doing it so they
        dont change me

i write these poems
so they dont
change
            me

so they dont
take
           my
           humanity

80.

there was a time
in my life
i thought about being
a journalist

        i remember
        hearing
        the university
        they called x
        —because it was named
        after a man who
        supported
        our genocide—
        was the best one
        to go to

i remember
imposter syndrome
i was never the
lead goal scorer
always on the bench
even though my grades
were good
i decided on less
competitive fields
in a less
competitive school

        what made
        the idf soldier
        turned journalist
        believe she
        could write
        for the
        new york
        times?

i watched a film
about republican
news sources
that show
too about
the morning news

        about
        the corruption
        the abuse
        the men wanting
        women
        in short
        skirts

lied to at every corner
and journalistic integrity
means nothing in this
world where the people
reporting on the
crimes committed by
brown bodies
are lying

they are lying we knew
they were lying and yet
when any of us asked
questions the institutions
were thrown in our faces
these myth makers these
names the times the post
its all lies i remember
wondering why my
grandma liked those
newspapers the ones with
the aliens the ones that
had JonBenét Ramsey on
the cover for years

the other day i told
students

*soon we wont be able to know
what the truth is*

i was refering to ai
but i am realizing
more and more
they tricked me
too

even with all my degrees
and my critical thinking
i wanted to believe in the
truth in the goodness of
people i wanted to
believe it was complex i
wanted to believe we
would never see this kind
of violence but here we
are and
we know the truth
your lies cant erase the
images we have
seen

81.

every inch is a victory

>> *take heart*
>> *we did not shut up*
>> *for six months*

we will not stop
we will
not stop

>>> *we will*
>>> *not stop*

i told the cbc
i hope every day
i pray every day
that the children in Gaza
live i pray and weep and
hope that i will wake up
to a permanent ceasefire
to a solution where
nobody else dies and
where people have food
and water and shelter

>> i said
> in the interview
>> i hope

i pray
every day
that the children
are fed

>> that i dont
> need to write
>> another
>> poem

but
i told you

> *if it keeps going—god forbid*
>> *if it keeps going*
> *i am prepared to commit*
>> *my lifetime*

i will remember them
i will tell
the children
of my
many niblings

>> *free pah le steen*

i will tell them i saw their
parents post photos of
them at the marches and
singing songs as you
coloured with your
crayons

>>> i will tell them
>>> of the poets
>>> of the little
>>>> girls

i will tell them of
the hospitals and the
libraries

i will tell them the stories
of how the empires fell and
the earth burned and we
committed everything we
had we changed everything
about our lives we did
something

>> *anything everything*[14]

82.

the song i
played the most
this year

am i proud of
listening to more
audiobooks
than music?

am i proud
of having a good
portion
of independent artists
on my list?

am i
ashamed
like years before
to share this
list?

i dont listen to that much music

the truce
has ended

like treaty
it didnt really mean
much
in the end
anyways

they are always
looking to
say how good they
do
how right
they are

and then they
continue the
genocide
oppression

our life expectancies
have lowered

and i wonder
what a genocide does
to the life expectancy
in Palestine

                              i try to
                           hold on to
                        some semblance
                              of joy

                          try to find
                          restoration
                             in my
                          relationships

                            visiting
                        resting my body
                        checking the app
                     for my favourite song

                          trying to sing
                        the shame away
                          remembering
                             always
                           Palestine

                        change is coming
                         change is here
                          we must keep
                           committed
                          to changing
                           this world

83.

listen to music
made by Palestinians

                    a song posted
                        from 2001
in 2001
i was
thirteen

                    i remember
            when the planes
                        came   *there have been*
            the buildings   *a thousand*
                        fell   *thousand*
            the people   *september*
                    jumped   *elevenths*

                                    my friend tells me

amazing to me now
to think of all those
living   of course
fighting   we arent used to
to survive   the bombs falling
to live   here

            is it just part of   but what about
            western culture   when they dont send a
                to jump?   fire truck to save babies
                to numb?   on the rez because of an
                to look   unpaid bill?
                  away?   what about
                                                our friend
                                                fundraising for
                                                    lifesaving
                                                    treatment?
                                    what about
                                    when a comedian
                                    makes a joke
                                    about the serial killer
                                    who preyed upon our
                                    women?

this week we are coming
together to talk about
language

        i am thinking about
          those old photos
           with a stack of
          relatives bones

a proud white man with a
gun posing for a photo
beside them

          they starved us
        by mass murdering
         our relations

i think of what they did
to me

        growing up ashamed
          of our languages
           our beadwork
            our dances
         our colourful ways
              of being
          in this world   what i see in Palestine is
                      the resistance—the kind
                      we only hear of in old
                      old stories but i know its
                                the same spirit

                            they cannot take
                    our pride in who we are
                              any longer
              your children
              will dance with your flag

                    just as ours will learn to
                          speak Ktunaxa

84.

i dont know what
to do
anymore   *feel so*
                                 broken and
                                         lost
donate
online   wonder
                           if the money
                                 helps
                           flip through
                            the stories

last night ka ha¢a *my uncle*
stood up to speak after i did
my keynote and played our
films on grief and he told us
we must prepare—
                         —*for the grief*
                                that is
                              to come
when the pandemic
became what it did
four years ago
this month
                            i remember
                      laughing at a post
                    calling it *the tiger king*
                           apocalypse
i remember
all the comments
we knew it was coming
we didnt think it would be so
boring

what of the collapse we are
witnessing now? what of sex
trafficking rings and one
point six mile bridges falling
into the water below?

what of the casualties being
migrant workers? what of the
police cities? what of the
blood on their hands? what
of black and brown bodies
everfacing the worst of it?

ka ha¢a *my uncle*
when he stood up
he talked of the
changing climate

                              he talked of
                              Christianity

and was sure to tell us
we must turn to the old ways
we cant be fighting using
those colonial beliefs we must
remember our spirits we will
need the old ways to help us
with what is to come i know
what he sees for we feel it
too—those of us who may
have gone by other names
centuries ago—the prophets
the witches the medicine
people we are witnessing we
are feeling it some of us
dreamed it before it got here
and we know we know the
new world is coming may the
old world inform it may
we all get ready may we all
remember the love as we
prepare for the grief that is
here

                          for the grief
                                that is
                              to come

85.

a young boy
carrying the body
of his
little brother
to the hospital
in his backpack
                    the kids
              are supposed to
                  be carrying
                       books
              in their backpacks
                    to school
to
school

and today i am thinking of
the elders who went to those
places they called schools
here where they were starved
where they were beaten
where they were buried in
unmarked graves where they
were subject to sexual abuses
we lower our voices when we
talk about that part last week
we gathered together to speak
our language the one they
tried to beat from our mouths

          i told the cbc
        i sometimes write
            two poems

              if the first one
               isnt hopeful
                  enough

these days i just feel crazy

       sometimes i question
                  everything

was all that real?
the ways i learned to pray?
the ways i learned to
think?
in hallways and
classrooms and between
book covers?

          would you believe me
                  if i told you
           im not even sure books
                        matter
                     anymore?

     what good is a book
  when a backpack is used
    to carry a childs body?

what good
a shelf
blown to pieces
pages scattered
across
the yard

what good
is any of it
the systems
institutions
money

there is still
something in me
that feels good
about my credit
score

even while the children
are dying and i find myself
disgusted at the ways i
am complicit i find myself
unable to move or organize
i find myself trying to grasp
even a tiny piece of ledge to
cling to but it seems like no
matter where i turn there
is another meeting another
committee another trigger
another story and i keep
repeating

free free Palestine

as i wash the dishes

save Gaza
let them live

as i clean the house

i dont know how to be in a
world where they are
starving

as i prepare
a meal

86.

and after you write that
last poem you see a post
warning about nihilism
and apathy

      you want to remind
          your readers
    you share how you feel
         in a moment

you want to feel
hopeful
believe this book will
matter because it signifies
sustained
effort

                  for yes
                  i may feel
                  in this capitalist
                  state
  you write   that a book
    for them   has become
because of the call   a product
  from Palestinians

speak of us tell our stories do
not forget us do not give up do
not stay silent make art write
poems
                        but then
                     i remember
                the first books
                 i read by
              native people

          i remember
          the instructions
          our late mother
          left behind
          in her
          writing
                  instructions
                that helped me
          when my now husband
             was fighting
              for his life

i post the last poem
and the next thing i see
is a picture
of moccasins
a story
from the
beader
the creator
the maker

            she reminds us
    that there is medicine in
                    trusting
            the process

do not mistake
my questioning
for apathy

my questioning leads to a
renewed trust every time
i ask
        what does it matter?   *it has to matter*

it helps me find
                    conviction   it matters in all the ways
                                        we cant know where the
                                        road will take us it
                                        matters because we are
                                        learning to sustain to
                                        change to refuse to look
                                        away to grieve to pray to
                                        hope to believe we are
                                        changing this world we
                                        can change this world we
                                        will we do we have
                                        before we can again

                                        remember remember
                                        remember
                                        love

87.

on land day
we gathered
mercury retrograde
had the zoom link all wild
and yet
we breathed together
waited
prayed
found our ways to
each other

            when i went
             to talk to
      nation members
           who were
        coming home
        i didnt feel
      i had the right
          words
             yet

        i never knew about
           land day
          before this
         before 2024

years ago
we talked with the
elders—*what would you say*
to someone returning?

a day to honour our relationship
to land by doing something for
it—a day Palestinians planted
olive trees—an idea a seed that
finds its way across the world
and back around again all of
us Indigenous people recognize
as we call land back land back
as we work to make the lakes
places the salmon will come
home to as we worry about snow
pack and wildfires as we listen
to the earth as we cry for her

        welcome home
      they said in english

but the other day
after we had them look at
old photographs

        (just saw a study
        about how old
        photographs
      calm our nervous
          systems)

we came up with a phrase
and it feels like such a
strong phrase it could
help us just knowing it

      sukni kin ɬawakiy
   ʔamakʔis ka·knik̓namunaɬa

sukni kin ƚawakiy
ʔamakʔis ka·kniknamunaƚa

its good you are here
on the lands
of our relatives/ancestors

this is why
land day

        this is why
        land back

this is how we understand
our connections and if
weve been displaced if
weve been moved we
always yearn for home and if
we are called to protect this
place of our ancestors we
will die upon this land so
that we are tied to it
forever for the next lifetime
and that is what i know and
pray

        that
        every living
Palestinian gets to survive
and know the land their
grandparents planted trees
on that every person alive
moves closer to
relationship with ʔamak
the land

and that every dear soul
martyred comes back down
to earth to a free Palestine
tastes the oil from trees
planted by their childrens
children

        because they survived

153

88.

a close friends mom died
right after her grandfather
feels like not even a week
went by between them

             an old colleague
             of our late mom
     posted that her dad died
and then her mom died too
             not even a week
                 went by
             between them

i missed a call from my
dad the other day
when i called him back
he said he was laying in the
grass in the sun feeling like
if he died right then it was
okay   and then
             he reminded me
             of a story
             my grandma
             his mom
          was in a nursing home
             in the end
             her sister
               too

these two old white women
lived in the same building
ate in the same rooms when
all the clients or patients
or community members
or whatever they call them
came together for meals
these two old women—
sisters—had dementia so
neither knew the other one
in conscious waking life

            my great aunt olive
               passed first
my grandma
followed her older sister
one last time—
             only four hours later
               not even a day
                  went by
             between them
and theres
this echo i keep hearing
words i had never heard
strung together in quite this
way before

          entire bloodlines
          ended

i suppose this happened to
us too   i mean
         we know there are
            some tribes
            that they call
            extinct
entire bloodlines

with one dropped bomb
rocket drone made to kill
they are saying now they
created weapons that are
trained through ai to fire
when the person enters
their homes or when they
are sleeping with their
families their families their
entire families gone

            not even a second
               went by
            between them

89.

something in me
broke   al shifa
                         bulldozers
              "where's daddy"

something in me
                         broke
the way
my new friends
eyes looked
on our last
call
              something in me
                         broke

seeing the horses being
used against the people in
downtown toronto

i wrote
half this poem
yesterday

                    this morning
          when i return to it
              i remember
          being twenty three
              i remember
          being in downtown
                    vancouver
              during the
          "stanley cup riots"

i remember just last week
driving to the end of our
road to where return out on
to the highway and a handful
of folks with "canadian" flags
were out there "protesting" the
carbon tax

                    back in 2011
              i wrote a post
          asking why young (old)
                    white men
              were "like this"

out in the streets lighting
cop cars on fire because of
a hockey game (out on the
highway with their flags
and their trucks fighting
against a tax that amounts
to how much really in a year?)

when cbc interviewed me
i tried to remind them
(teach them)
                         were not
                         protestors
us
out in the streets
begging for an end
to the genocide
screaming for a free
Palestine

                              us
              we see ourselves
                    as protectors
              fighting for life
              fighting for life
              fighting against
                         death
we are here to
become the prayer
and when i think of these
differences i feel something
in me
breaking
breaking
                    broken

90.

six months of genocide
i wonder what
six months into
the arrival
after 1492
felt like

      no
      wait
     more like
    six months
    into 1567

          coming on
           seventy
              six
            years
             of
        occupation
            plus
              six
         months

today marks nine months
weve been married we
chose the seventh for so
many different reasons
but none of me could
have imagined we would
share this anniversary date
with the beginning of so
much death

           last night
my husband took me
      on a date night
        he bought us
      tickets to a most
          incredible
              show

black and rural
shayna jones
interviewed forty Black
and rural artists makers
tree talkers lovers of the
land and solitude

years ago
i was awakened
to the concept of
global
Indigeneity
without thought of race

          do you know
     the dna difference
between people from
         different
     countries in africa
is more diverse than
      the difference
between black and white
            skin?

i wonder
about genetics
between
Palestinians and
their colonizers

over here i am part of two
nations that are deeply
linked by dna—we are all
family—and yet when the
colonial mindset shows
up we see the ways we
begin to fight each other
for the scraps   may we
all learn
                from Palestine
to take care of each other

may we learn from
shayna to talk to the trees

        may there still be trees
        left in Palestine to help
                the healing

may this army leaving the
ground leave for good
and not be preparing for
further air strikes

this is the ninetieth poem
i have written in six
months the goal was one
hundred and now i
wonder how many more
poems?
                how many more
                        months?

        all i know is we will meet
                them all—each day
                —until they are
                        free—
                        —until
                                we
                                all
                                are

91.

in my dreams
i was at some weird
dive bar kinda place
about to read
poetry
                    everyone
                was drinking
                the poet that
                    opened
                        was
                doing some
                fluff poems
                    sweet
                and nice
                    and
                spoken wordy

                        the front of the stage
                        became the street

the band
that was to come on
after me   i was performing
decided theyd set up   for people walking by
their gear and wait   like a busker
behind me
so i felt crowded at the   when i opened my mouth
front of the stage   to read my first
                                        poem

                        the toronto police
                        showed up
                                as if me saying
                                    Palestine
                                beckoned them

                        they stood there in their
                        riot gear and i finished
                        my poem
                                i called them out
                                for being there
                                for bothering us
                        the poets

and then i decided to read
the sexy poems the
crowd pleasers the ones
that make you laugh

> but in this dream
> as i flipped through
> my book
> i couldnt find
> the pages
> i couldnt find
> the poems

what i know
from this dream
from others

> this eclipse
> season
> is helping me
> shed skin

i am changing
i hope you
are changing   may we
            all   be changed

> may we never again
> silence ourselves
> feel nervous
> choose the safety
> of minimizing or hiding
> or
> letting
> the cops
> scare us into
> reading a
> different
> poem

92.

how do i say it? *ide?*

eed

eid mura—
                    —eid mubarak

eid mubarak!

yes!

we talk about how
we hated our
brown skin
when we were
younger   we share
                    of our language
                    our foods
                    our medicines

i think of our own
greeting during our new years

ki?suk kyukyit
ku·kinmakut
                    (good day
                    one more
                    year)
Eid Mubarak
                    (blessed
                    feast)

and this morning i see Bisans
post i read her
words i see her eyes

                    Gaza is the
                    most beautiful place
                    on earth

we will rebuild even if it takes
one hundred years

even after she shares
every day is a nightmare
that when the army
retreats she runs to find
anything left of her
real
life

even while Jenan asks

how do you celebrate holy
days when there are no
children to celebrate?

and i am brought back to an
image i carry close something
the elders taught me
                    a story from
                    back in that place
                    they called a
                    "school"

(that place they took our
                    children to—
                    —the place of unmarked
graves and sexual abuse and
being beaten for speaking our
                    languages)

the kids hid away in the
dark at new years time to
secretly hold our
ceremonies
                    resistance
                    resist
we will rebuild
                    we will bring
                    the children
                    home

93.

i walked to the river
got out of my car
and a bird called out
bringing me to
tears of gratitude

i walked to the water
knowing this
lifeblood
connects us
me
to
Gaza
to you
to the north
to the south
to the sea
and back
again
i put my medicines
in the river
imagine what comes next
say
im listening

almost immediately
look at my phone
realize
and put it back
in my pocket

dont lie to them
if you say you are
listening

listen

no
really

listen

hear a small
splashing
hear the river
flow

so much
quieter
than it should be

i think
anyways
cant really
remember
last year

but the snow pack
was low
the water
is low
and yet still
¢ikku
finds a spot
to clean herself
her red orange breast
the first sign of spring

reminds me of the poppy
Bisan found reminds me
of the children waiting to
hear the birds sing
wishing for their own
water to bathe in to drink
to sit by in the
quiet peace of a free
Palestine

94.

stay focused

the moon is squaring
neptune
my astrology app
tells me
and i am seeking
information
about Iran
scroll through
posts saying
the drones have stopped
the buzzing has stopped
others saying
it has not
they are still
martyring
learn about
the government
in Iran
see biden and
trudeau
come out again
supporting
iz ray el

find
voices
from Iran

scroll through their posts
only to find a chart

outlining why being
pro
pah le steen
is
not
a
"solution"

the thing about being a
survivor of genocide in a
brown body is that i am
going to understand and
witness a genocide on
brown bodies differently
than one of my best
friends white dads but i
have to be honest here
and say

i am learning
i am unsure

the thing about
white supremacy
white governments
white nationalism
(white dads)

the decisions
made to strike to defend
happen fast in dark
locked down rooms
(i imagine)

                    is that
                urgency
            is the game

and no matter what
                    we
            the people
                suffer

they tell us theres no
other way and thats the
part i wont be confused
about thats the part i cant
let stand there has to be
there is we can imagine we
can birth it we can be
another way another way
another way

i dont know what it all
means but i do know
we must
become
another
way

95.

we must
be

          come
          another
          way

the war we thought would end
in just a matter of days

wake to the news
of one year of war
in Sudan
only six days
before your own
solar return

      you are preparing
           to turn
           thirty six

the astrologers say thirty six is
an important year as we move
out of a difficult thirty fifth
(twelfth house profection) year
and back into the first house
back rising over the horizon
line (ascendant) and becoming
ourselves again

twelve year cycles
the last time
jupiter
went in to
gemini
i finished my
masters

please
let this
mean
i will
complete
this other
degree—

       and yet
what do papers
and lines on a page
really mean?

when there has been a year of
death chaos and destruction
in Sudan when there has
been six months of genocide
in Palestine when i grew up
hearing lies from white men
when i grew up watching
them tell us on tv that they
would keep us safe when that
man touched you when you
were twelve and your dad
said he called the guy and
you said

you shoulda killed him

164

there are eleven
Ktunaxa covenants
do not commit murder   is listed fourth

and when
our elders
included
the covenants
as part of our
strategic plan

someone
suggested
changing it
to
do no harm

this is how we see the
reality watered down by
people who cant believe
things get this bad those
who arent like us but
want to suggest we change
our words

and all i can think of is
what about the warriors
who had to take a life what
about the ones who found
themselves starved and
beaten and

today
is a day
of action
today i pray
for those taking
on
the world

we must
be
come
another
way

96.

famine
and
houselessness
and
empowered
police
states

        we watched
     this documentary
      about a cult
       in oregon

there are no Indigenous
people here
they say

the white people
interviewed
mad that others
had taken over
"their" lands
"their" town

not knowing
that we have a name
for every place
we have memory

      no mention
      anywhere
      that they
     had done the
     very same
       to us

        there is
       controversy
       right now
      all over the
local facebook groups
      about a train
       an old
       historic
       train

whiteness and catholicism
its own cult that displaced
and murdered and starved
our people until they forgot
we ever existed at all

sure

      they say its
     about labour
       and
      unions

but i cant help it
all i hear is folks
wanting to preserve

      colonial
      history

they find themselves
up in arms
writing letters
our mla
committed
to saving
the train
the fort
the fort
named for the settler
that bought up
all the land here
that helped
put us on
reserves
that
helped
send us to
those
"schools"

do i sound like an angry ndn?
because i am because that
fort is a celebration of your
history colonizing our people
and i have to trust have to
believe that a hundred years
from now there will be no
fort iz ray el in Palestine i
have to believe we can turn it
around

i have to hold
my unpopular opinions
that the fort
should be returned
to our people

land back
from here
to there
land back land back
every
where

97.

wake up
its been more than
seven years
since you drank
alcohol
and yet
here you are
feeling
hungover

this world
moves
too fast
this world
moves
too
fast

yesterday spinning

you are thinking
about sustainability
about screen time
and the ways in which
this constant
dopamine
rush

takes us
into
or out
of
relationship

spinning

everything foggy
in my brain
the sun was out
in the morning
and then it hailed
snowed on the
mountains

as you get
closer to your
goal

you are thinking
about healing
you are thinking about
losing your mind
you are thinking about

one
hundred
poems

how things
change
or do they?

yesterday
you met
with someone
who is willing to
help
yesterday
you also
visited
your mentor
(friend)
                          yesterday you
                          made a choice

too much too much youre
doing too much and what
happens when you do too
much you stop being able
to decipher what is good
or bad right or wrong how
your actions align with your
values how you can stay   we keep going
connected to your instincts   *trust*
when all you want to do is   *your*
crawl in a hole what is this   *gut*
incessant call to avoid hide
move away from anything   and if you cant
you said yes to? how do you   get clear
keep going? what do we do?
what do we do? what do we   step
do?
                                           away
                                  go to
                                           the river

                          listen—

                          until you know yourself
                                          again

98.

a playground
a playground
a playground

                they
           bombed
              a
            play
          ground

the ground where we play
think of the long grasses
the tall firs the way we
would walk across the
field to the bus stop just
little kids we werent
scared of anything falling
from the sky we werent
scared we didnt have to
be

          a playground
             a play
          ground
             a
          play ground

my husband
works with
kids

its something i
love about him

hes not
afraid
hes not
afraid

when i had to borrow his
truck once i drove past
the
play
ground

the play ground
the
play
ground

one of "his" (all of our)
kids started running
across the playground

the playground
        the playground!

the kid was yelling the
name they call my
husband and running
across the playground and
when i called out to him
and waved saying it was
me you could see him
stop in shock

                smokii
                stole
                your
                truck!

these are the only stories
about playgrounds i want
to tell

i want to tell you
we called one playground

                (the
        playground!)

adventureland
with its rubber chips and
chain bridge

        we called another
            bongoland
        that one had a   the   playground   the
            big slide   playground they bombed
                                and killed the children on
                                the playground

                                THE PLAYGROUND!

99.

all day
driving around
here
to there

        every day
        as i am
        out
        there

i find myself pretending
that i am okay sitting in
meetings on a screen in
my car use a hot spot to
connect then drive home
pick up the dog and take
him to the vet to get him
vaccines so he can keep
going to the kennel
going to the playcare so
your husband can drive
him there and you can
scroll socials

        feeling
        worse
        and
        worse

sometimes my body is like ice
sometimes i fall into a sleep
with my body still clenched
unable to speak move i am
numb i am not real none of
this can be real am i am i
sometimes i scream and yell
and the dog looks nervous and
i feel awful so awful about
how i cant contain everything
this witnessing has grown in
me this anger this rage this
ripping of my mind and heart
from a reality that forgets you
Palestine

oh Palestine
                    and
                  worse
               and worse   the pain in my body
                                   the realizations i am
                                   making about what
                                   processed foods and
                                   refined sugar are doing to
                                   me

           the recognition
           that everything
           that brings us
                  comfort
            comes at the
              expense of
               someones
                    life   the life
                               of someones
                               child

                               delete the apps delete the
                               apps delete the apps if
                               even for a few hours just
                               write two more poems
                               two more poems is it only
                               two   more
                               before day 45 you never
                               considered   youd   be
                               writing 100 poems there
                               was something in you
                               hopeful and now there is
                               just   this
                               the commitment to two
                               more poems and just
                               one more after this
                               last line

                                             one
                                            more
                                       will make
                                    one hundred

100.

one hundred poems
      for Palestine
one
hundred and
ninety six
days
      since october seventh

twenty four
poems
faxed to the
prime minister
      less calls than that
         if im honest
one racist
email reply
from the elected
official
in my riding   three
         shirts
         purchased
         from artists
hundreds
of dollars sent
to mutual aid   two
         books
         mailed
         to raffle winners

      one
      keffiyeh
      worn

something like
three songs sung
at each of four prayer
gatherings

      thirty five years
      walking on this earth

seventy six years
of occupation

five hundred thirty two
      years of colonization

      fifty four years
      since they closed
      kootenay
      indian
      residential
      school
thirty seven years
since ka titi was
murdered
(thirty seven years
after she was born)

      thirty three thousand
seven hundred and ninety
      Palestinians martyred

fourteen thousand
children

      seventy six thousand
      seven hundred and
      seventy Palestinians
      wounded

millions suffering famine
starvation
lack of medication
grief upon grief upon
grief

      one hundred
      poems
      for
      Palestine

may we see an end before
i write one hundred more

ACKNOWLEDGEMENTS

First and foremost, I am grateful to Palestinian people and the Palestinian resistance for their heart and dedication to each other and to their homelands.

I am grateful to my good friend, poet and muralist Zaynab Mohammad, who has walked beside me fiercely and gently throughout this time—Zaynab, as best I can, I am listening.

To my editor, Jazz, thank you for holding this work with so much care. Thank you for the disability intimacy, the grace, compassion and watchful eye that wouldn't let me give up. This book is here because of you.

Thank you to those who provided endorsements for this book. Omar, Catherine, Maral, Rayya, we are in this together. Thank you for always reminding me we are not alone.

To all those who read, resonated, liked, shared and commented on the original poems, or messaged me to connect, thank you for reminding me of the "why" of it all every time you reached out in solidarity.

And truly, I must thank the poets. Those targeted, those writing from tents and shelters, those of the diaspora. Thank you for reminding me of who I am. May the poets always see clearly. May we always speak up.

ENDNOTES

1   Crown-Indigenous Relations and Northern Affairs Canada, "Statement of apology to former students of Indian Residential Schools," *Canada.ca*, June 11, 2008. rcaanc-cirnac.gc.ca/eng/1100100015644/1571589171655.

2   Shree Paradkar, "RCMP's dastardly defiling of reconciliation on Wet'suwet'en lands cannot be undone," *Toronto Star,* February 10, 2020. thestar.com/opinion/star-columnists/rcmp-s-dastardly-defiling-of-reconciliation-on-wet-suwet-en-lands-cannot-be-undone/article_5b8db45b-b272-5e43-9b36-cb462a5fb5a9.html

3   Jeff Shantz, "Canadian police connections with Israel colour responses to Palestinian Solidarity," *GreenLeft,* October 13, 2023. https://www.greenleft.org.au/content/canadian-police-connections-israel-colour-responses-palestinian-solidarity.

4   Ktunaxa Nation Council, "Ktunaxa Statement of Reconciliation," *Ktunaxa Nation,* September 28, 2021. ktunaxa.org/?s=statement+of+reconciliation.

5   Danielle Pradis, "First Nations life expectancy plummets in Alberta due to opioid deaths," *APTN News,* July 4, 2023. https://www.aptnnews.ca/national-news/first-nations-life-expectancy-plummets-in-alberta-due-to-opioid-deaths/.

6   Wikipedia, "Steven Salaita hiring controversy," September 24, 2024. en.wikipedia.org/wiki/Steven_Salaita_hiring_controversy.

7   Lee Maracle, Talking to the Diaspora (Winnipeg: ARP Books, 2015).

8   Queering the Map @queeringthemap, "This 4th of July we are thinking about the fact that the U.S.A. is the biggest supplier of arms to Israel," *Instagram,* July 4, 2024. instagram.com/p/C9AqS2YR1Og/.

9   Cosmic Apps Pty Ltd, "Pluto in Scorpio," *Astrogold,* Version 8.0.4, https://www.astrogold.io/, date accessed Oct 2 2024.

10   Quill Christie Peters @raunchykwe, "Sharing some of my words from yesterday/first and foremost, Anishinaabeg stand with Palestine. Indigenous peoples across Turtle Island stand with Palestine," *Instagram,* October 26, 2023. https://www.instagram.com/p/Cy4XOFrrJBo/?img_index=1.

11   Tareq S. Hajjaj, "This Could Be My Last Report From Gaza. Keep My Stories Alive," *Truthout,* October 16, 2023. truthout.org/articles/this-could-be-my-last-report-from-gaza-keep-my-stories-alive/.

12   Ktunaxa Nation Council, "Ktunaxa Statement of Reconciliation."

13   King, Thomas. *The Truth About Stories.* House of Anansi Press Inc, 2003.

14   Dimaline, Cherie. *The Marrow Thieves,* Cormorant Books, 2017.